Care. Share.
Be your best.
from Paul

Kim
1-1-2006

THE REAL
RAIN MAN

Kim Peek

by his father
Fran Peek

Edited by Stevens W. Anderson

Harkness
Publishing Consultants LLC

Harkness Publishing Consultants LLC
P.O. Box 27611
Salt Lake City, Utah 84127-0611

Library of Congress # 96-076374

Second Edition
Printed in the United States of America

ISBN 0-9651163-0-1

This book carries an invitation . . .

. . . to share a journey with Kim Peek,
the remarkable "megasavant"
who was screenwriter Barry Morrow's
inspiration for the Oscar-winning movie
Rain Man . . .

. . . to gain an increased awareness of
the great potential within each of us
and to better realize that all
have a gift to give,
some contribution to make . . .

. . . to spend a little time with Kim
as he travels to Hollywood
to meet with megastar Dustin Hoffman,
whose on-screen character Raymond Babbitt
touched the hearts of millions of people
around the world . . .

. . . to come to know,
through a collection of personal anecdotes,
quips and "media megabytes,"
Kim's "private side" . . .

. . . and to witness his seasoning as,
day by day, he ventures further and further
out into the world.

**It will be a journey you'll never forget.
Happy reading!**

Contents

APPENDIX

Acknowledgments

This book is dedicated to
Kim's mother,
Jeanne,
his brother Brian
and his sister Alison,
all who love him dearly and
for whom I can't begin to express
adequate appreciation.

Special thanks also to
Kim's Aunt Phyllis P. Black,
Terry Peek and his family,
and Mary Ruth "Gold Tooth" Haslam
for their encouragement and support in making
the real world Kim's world, too.

And our sincere gratitude to Ellen Smith,
Irma and Stan Evans, Kim's wonderful tutors,
and to Anya Seton Chase, his favorite author.

Of course, without the kind encouragement of
Barry Morrow, Dustin Hoffman, Tom Cruise,
Barry Levinson, Mark Johnson,
and all those who worked in and behind the scenes
in the making of *Rain Man*,
none of this could have come about.

And thanks, too, to the thousands of new friends
who have helped nurture the self-esteem and confidence
of this very special person.

PREFACE

In the movie *Rain Man*, Charlie Babbitt (Tom Cruise), a financially strapped hot-shot dealer in foreign cars, is stunned. His father has just died and left his entire three million-dollar estate, not to Charlie, but to Charlie's autistic older brother Raymond (Dustin Hoffman). Why, Charlie wasn't even aware he *had* a brother!

In a grab for his rightful piece of the inheritance, Charlie snatches the confused Raymond from the asylum where he's lived most of his life. From there the two head west cross-country to Los Angeles, where Charlie works. In their travels, Charlie slowly decelerates from his fast-lane thinking and not only comes to love his brother but to realize that he manifests some special gifts: Ray's not retarded, he's a savant. . .

The *real-life* "Rain Man" isn't autistic; on the contrary, now that he's come out among people he's very outgoing. Nor is he a mere savant—he's a *mega*savant, with a wide range of knowledge and abilities. For that matter, in many ways the "real Rain Man" may be even *more* remarkable, *more* awe-inspiring than his screen character.

FOREWORD

When I first met Kim, he touched me on the shoulder and told me so many things about myself—my phone number, for instance, all about my home town, and all the television programs I had been involved in. But more than that, he told me to 'think about myself.' It's a challenge that I've continued to try to do.

At the same time I've continued to think about Kim and what was formerly the kind of confined world which he lived in, a sort of prison that was created by the fact that he was unable to really venture out into the world. He loved his many books and shared the lives of the people and characters who lived within their covers.

And while he has now been able to bring that world out to many people by lecturing to and interacting with tens of thousands of people, especially children and young people around the country, a curious thing has happened to Kim: the bars of his prison have begun to fall aside and out has emerged not just a marvelously gifted human being, but a warm, compassionate, caring person who defies the labels of 'autism' and 'mental retardation.'

In the past few years, since the movie *Rain Man* received its four Oscars in March of 1989, Kim has become not only an outstanding role model for persons with disabilities, but a sign of hope to parents and families and a true inspiration to me and to countless others. I don't think anybody could spend five minutes with Kim and not come away with a slightly altered view of themselves, the world, and our potential as human beings.

I say to you, Kim, my dear and special friend, that watching your growth, your journey through life, and watching you, Fran, who is always there to guide him and to stand in the shadows when necessary to allow Kim to have the limelight for himself, is a wonderful testament to love, to our infinite capacity to grow, as well as to the extraordinary, unknown boundaries of our own minds and what we might do with Kim's unique example.

Barry Morrow
Screenwriter of *Rain Man*

PART I

AN INVITATION TO MEET KIM

Come On In!

A FEW LIGHT SNOWFLAKES DRIFT DOWN FROM A WHITE, afternoon sky. Inside, a library patron sporting a black, purple, and gray Colorado Rockies jacket impatiently mills up and down along the spacious shelves. He meanders into the "closed" reference sections behind the library staff desks, seeking out a specific book. Every now and then, his mouth, drawn outward like the slats of a horizontal blind, broadens into an enthusiastic grin as he happens upon a book he hasn't yet explored.

His pacing quickens. He's in his comfort zone, very much at home in this, one of his favorite haunts, amid this throng of regular patrons and library staff (all of whom know him well, watch over him, and are accustomed to his unbroken chatter). Yet at the same time he's also very much alone as he roams among the flow of strangers ranging from a well-dressed businesswoman to a ragged transient.

He's encased in his own world, a faraway preoccupation with books. Thinking aloud, mumbling to himself in soft undertones, he shuffles mechanically on down the aisle in his customary penguin-like gait, his dronings echoing faintly for yards around. "Or less . . . Or less," he repeats in a rhythmic delivery. Pausing in an awkward stance and picking up a familiar reference book, he chuckles, ticks off a series of numbers, then mutters to no one in particular, "You can check it out."

Finding an empty seat, he settles back with several massive catalogs he has collected in his wanderings. Gently spreading the pages of one of the volumes, he removes his black-rimmed, thick-lens glasses and places them on the table. Then he positions the elongated tip of his nose about six inches from the page, squints his eyes, and begins reading, exhaling audibly with each breath, a low, guttural engine-revving noise.

A half hour later he carefully replaces the catalogs and retreats to a narrow row of phone directories. Removing one of the thick volumes and opening his red three-ring notebook marked with his name in large block letters, he sits down and finds the spot where he left off the last time (the residents of Boise, Idaho—next week it might be an obscure town in Minnesota). The index finger of his right hand navigates precisely along a line of data, and he leans forward and to the right to let his left hand do its work. Deftly clutching a pencil, he begins neatly scratching out row after row of names, each followed by an address, city, state, ZIP code, and phone number—minutia not merely committed to the pages of a dollar notebook, but also to his own computerlike memory.

The minutes stretch into an hour, and finally his jottings cease. He hoists the directory back into its place and rambles off once more, this time beelining to a shelf filled with reference books to check out a thick work titled *Chronicle of the 20th Century.*

Settling into a nearby chair, he works his fingers upward in front of his face and gazes at and through them, a ritual repeated several times an hour. He opens the book and begins studying the happenings of the early 1900s. He pores over the pages swiftly, while occasionally mumbling a date or name. With each breath he emits a slightly new sound—a soft whistle, a whine, a high, throaty groan, or a low giggle.

In his seemingly erratic searchings, he comes across an article on Russia's "Bloody Sunday" of 1905 and peruses it in depth. Then, between soft, higher-pitched groans, he slowly begins citing a list of dates: "February 24th, March 6th, April 7th . . ."

The fact-packed pages flip over about every thirty seconds. "June 24th (groan) . . . July 15th . . ." Every now and then he quizzes himself on a date or place, the answers spilling from his lips as if he's taking an open-book quiz and the answer is right in front of him (though by then he's turned several pages beyond that particular bit of information).

He turns back to his work and almost advances to the next page when something catches his eye: "August 17th." And finally, jiggling his knees and stamping his feet in delight, he announces "September 10th!"—then skips forward to the year 1906, pleased at his accomplishment.

The routine continues, the pages turning one after another, his head cocked to the side like a robin listening for a worm: "January 29th . . . April 19th . . . San Francisco earthquake . . . June 10th, 1910 . . . July 17th . . . school children . . . August 22nd . . . Mona Lisa stolen . . ."

Now delicately fingering the page, a faint moan slowly rises into a deep chuckle—followed by minute upon minute of silence. His head swivels back and forth along the pages, his eyes tracking one historical fact after another. His bottom lip protrudes in a permanent pout and he shakes his right hand every now and again as if emptying his body of its excess buildup of energy.

Finally another chuckle rumbles from deep in his throat, once again setting in motion a series of mumblings and browsings. Minutes later, with the wide crease of a smile spreading over his face, he cries out in simple triumph, "April threeeeee!"

Here is clearly a man who loves learning—for its own sake.

Then, just like that, the search changes course. He's unearthed—perhaps out of something he just read or something he read months ago—a certain month and day: November 8th. But since it appears that the exact year eludes him, he begins flipping pages and scanning down each year's "Summary of Events," whispering some dates under his breath, letting out others as if greeting a long-lost friend, until he comes across the year: 1923, Hitler is arrested after a failed coup attempt.

Roughly three hours have elapsed since he first climbed from the car and ambled through the building's double doors—but still his eyes dart across the pages, his head with its thick mop of brown hair and occasional gray streak bowed in silence, swiveling up and down, side to side . . .

It's time for him to go home now. Finding him deep in his studies at one of his customary first-floor tables, I ask him what exactly it is he's looking for. "I start with a certain day and advance until there's nothing left over," he explains. "Just advancing…"

Meet Kim Peek, the "Real" Rain Man

WHEN YOU FIRST COME FACE TO FACE WITH THIS remarkable "megasavant," once considered mentally retarded, you might perceive him as rather self-centered and aloof, or perhaps brusque and unfeeling. In fact, if you didn't know Kim, some of his comments and responses to questions might even smack of conceit.

First appearances, however, can be deceiving.

After a few minutes, you will discover, as many have by now discovered, the real Kim: a man long on extraordinary mental abilities and a little short on social and motor skills; a man wholly engrossed in his studies; a quiet man who, fearful of stormy weather and new situations in general, prefers to be

by himself or in the company of close friends and family; a man who innocently assumes that everyone he meets knows as much as he does and is on the same wavelength as he is; a distractable man whose mind is tugged back and forth between the horde of intricate and colorful thoughts running through it; a man whose brain, like an ever-widening beam of light, can't help but focus on many ideas at once; a man who only in the past seven event-filled years is emerging as a "complete" adult. You will also come to understand that Kim is a man who finally is being given his due both as a savant possessing some 15 extraordinarily rare mental gifts and as an increasingly sensitive, tenderhearted, joy-filled individual who both needs others' love and affection and gives it in return. And Kim is also a man with a message to deliver, a man who has taken to heart his role as a late-blooming goodwill ambassador and zealous advocate for the disabled.

This book is only part of Kim's story, the story of his "late-blooming" and the emergence of his more public, outgoing self. As such, it contains a partial collection of stories about Kim, told as accurately as can be recollected. As you acquaint yourself with his meticulous and literal character, you will better understand the unusual phrases and language patterns he uses to express himself. I call these "one-liner" expressions sprinkled throughout the book KimKwips, quips and "turned-around" quotes—some poignant reminders of our common humanity, others whimsical expressions of our ofttimes laughable humanness—that suggest what Kim is all about and the person he's becoming.

Kim is definitely unique, though to him, he's pretty much like everyone else. As he describes himself, "I'm just a normal human male."

With that said . . . meet Kim!

Kim Is My Son

KIM IS A ONE-OF-A-KIND MEGASAVANT AND THE ORIGINAL inspiration for the Academy Award-winning motion picture *Rain Man*, released in 1988. But, more importantly, he is my son. And, though his loving mother (we have divorced, and she has since remarried) and his younger brother, Brian, and sister, Alison, remain a big part of his life, I'm his day-to-day caregiver—and his biggest fan.

KimKwip—A reporter once asked Kim, "Do you think you've been given a gift?" Characteristic of both his brain's distortions and his unassuming nature, Kim answered, "I've been given a gift from everyone I see."

Kim was born in Salt Lake City, Utah, on November 11, 1951 (a Sunday, Kim would quickly remind me). Although her pregnancy seemed reasonably normal, Kim's mother underwent a difficult labor preceding his birth.

From the beginning we knew he was "different." His head was 30 percent larger than normal, so large his neck muscles couldn't support it; he was sluggish and cried a lot; there was no play, no normal response to stimulus, no solid stages of development; each of his eyes moved independently of the other; and a soft, baseball-size blister stretched across the back of his head on the right side, a growth doctors refused to touch for fear that it might be a part of his brain. Later, at age three, the blister quickly retracted, at the same time pulling a

Kim, his mother Jeanne, me, Ali and Bri, 1961

nodule into Kim's cerebellum and destroying half of it.

At nine months a doctor pronounced Kim mentally retarded and recommended that we place him in an institution and "get on with your lives." We took him home.

Cuddled in our arms or lying there on the sofa with his head propped up with pillows, we read to him, hour after hour, tracing the rows of words with his tiny finger as we went. And, in time, our so-called "retarded" infant son began displaying some remarkable abilities. For one, he took an early interest in books, apparently absorbing everything he heard and saw.

At 18 months he showed marked signs of being a creature of habit. For instance, he always insisted on turning the Little

KimKwip—Visiting with the owner of a local farm house: "You ought to open the door so the flies can get out!"

Golden Books upside down once we read them to him to separate them from unread material, a habit he maintains even today. (The way he explains it now, if the content of a book or a magazine is already committed to his memory, he no longer needs to refer to it.)

Physically, he developed slowly—not learning to walk on his own until he was past four. But we always sensed that he possessed some special gift, some mental powers beyond our ability to explain. But it's only been fairly recently that we have come to appreciate how deep and far-reaching those powers are.

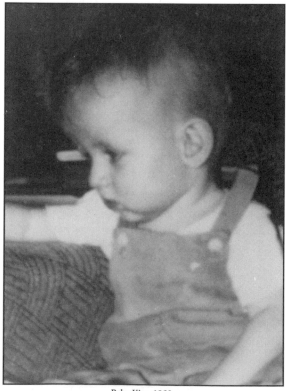

Baby Kim, 1952

The first real signs of Kim's unique gifts surfaced when he was three. One day when he was browsing through the newspaper, he came to me and asked, "Dad, what does 'con-fi-den-ti-al' mean?" Without thinking, I jokingly told him to look it up in the family dictionary. He did. About 30 seconds after putting his head down, crawling like a snowplow over to the desk, and pulling himself up, he found the word and read out the definition. We started watching him more carefully after that.

As a little boy, Kim never stopped reading—and memorizing—everything he could get his hands on, including phone directories, atlases, biographies, and histories. (It's estimated he's read some 7,600 books to this point, representing a staggering number of facts and figures. In my mind, without books and the stimulus they provide, Kim's life—like his cerebellum—would be shattered.)

The clincher came when we found he could recite, verbatim, whole paragraphs from a book at the mere mention of a page number. At six, he had memorized the entire index of a set of encyclopedias.

Posing on the stairway, 1959

When it came time for Kim to go to school, however, he was rejected due to his hyperactivity. He lasted a grand total of seven minutes in the classroom. Soon after, we were advised to consider him for a lobotomy, at the time an accepted way to control hyperactive or institutionalized individuals. We, of course, declined. (Kim still refers to one of the doctors who recommended the lobotomy as "the bastard"—a term, by the way, that for Kim conveys a turned-around and much kinder meaning than it would for you or me.)

Back at home we soon discovered that even though Kim was extremely introverted, often disruptive, and couldn't bathe or dress himself or brush his own teeth, he could, in addition to his reading, instantly add, subtract, and multiply numbers in his head. As time went on he even learned to multiply fractions and perform other moderately difficult math problems, all in his calculator-like brain.

When Kim was 12, a "mini coming out" took place. It was Christmas Eve, and the traditional crowd of relatives had gathered at his grandmother's home. In the middle of singing Christmas carols and the reciting of stories, Kim came to me and asked if he could take part in the program. Naturally we were thrilled to have him participate. And there, in a shy, soft voice, on what was to be for us a most holy night indeed, he stood before us and recited the entire Christmas story.

When he wasn't scouring the pages of a book, Kim liked to go for rides to read license plates and gaze at the scenery. He could identify a street corner solely by its street light. Encouraged, we arranged for teachers to come to our home for a few hours each week, and by age 14, Kim had completed his high school requirements.

Looking back, he must have been terribly frightened—frightened of the flood of tangled thoughts rushing through his head, destroying his ability to concentrate, and frightened

Kim tells the Christmas story, 1962

of the apparent unpredictability of outsiders compared to the fiercely protective love of his parents. So he retreated behind a safe, studious barrier of silence. And there he stayed, removed, sheltered, cloistered in his room. Because all he wanted to do was read, we didn't even know how to include him in family activities. For the most part, he remained a terribly withdrawn child.

Unlocking "Kimputer"

KIM WAS GIVEN HIS FIRST X-RAY BRAIN SCAN IN 1983 during a medical exam required by Medicaid—our only source for health protection since Kim is not health-care insurable through private plans because he was diagnosed "mentally retarded" at birth. Because scanning technology at that time was limited to radiation X-ray, only the bone areas could be seen on the negatives. During the exam, a neurologist identified Kim's single, integrated brain hemisphere, just one solid brain lobe, larger than normal, but he was unable to map out any other tissue areas. It appeared the lobes had actually been fused together, and it was assumed that his corpus callosum hadn't formed—a fact verified by later analysis. (The corpus callosum is a connective tissue

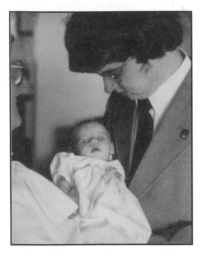

Kim with his niece at her blessing, 1979

segment of the brain that enables the two brain hemispheres to communicate with one another. Other recognized savants whose brains have been examined—Einstein's, Lenin's, Stalin's and others—boast larger than normal corpora callosa. Unlike these acknowledged geniuses, Kim has no corpus callosum whatsoever.)

A 1989 documentary by a local TV reporter included a fascinating study of Kim's brain using new Magnetic Resonance Imagery (MRI) technology, which has opened many doors to better understanding of how the brain functions. The comprehensive MRI analysis showed, among other things, that the right half of Kim's cerebellum had literally exploded into eight or nine small pieces, probably caused by extreme pressure when the swelling on the back of his head receded into his brain. The left side of the cerebellum is intact.

This "shattering" of the right side of his cerebellum, coupled with the fact that his brain cavity is more fluid than cortex and that he has no corpus callosum, account for most of his motor deficiencies. Many skills associated with normal living are beyond his ability to perform. Though he is able to handle most of his bathroom needs, Kim requires assistance in bathing, dressing, food preparation, tooth-brushing and hair-combing. While walking, he regularly has to be warned of upcoming stairs or changes in ground textures (i.e., concrete to asphalt, carpet to tile), or he will pause and try to step over and into the new texture. On occasion, he has fear of escalators that are going down.

However, though his motor deficiencies make it hard for him to participate in most activities which require body/mind coordination, he still has precise printing and cursive penmanship skills, can operate a television set and a record player, and is able to eat his food in a mannerly way.

Because the cerebellum helps coordinate the brain's governing of the motor system, the breakup of the right side of Kim's cerebellum may explain why messages sent to Kim's body from his brain are frequently either inconsistent or intercepted completely. Probability is about 40,000 to 1 that the eight or nine segments comprising his brain's right side will pass on the same message twice in a row. That's why his mind can unexpectedly catapult in any direction and onto any track, leaving a half-dozen or so other ill-fated thoughts dangling—perchance to be retrieved at a later time—and causing his unpredictable, confusing thought patterns and behavior. His inability to perform simple motor activities also could be partly due to this phenomena. This is a personal theory from extensive research and thinking I have done over the past few years. No medical conclusions have been suggested or determined.

Despite his mental and physical limitations, Kim's reservoir of knowledge and his recall capabilities are awesome. Several psychologists have likened him to a computer—and he enjoys from time to time being called "Kimputer."

Neuro-developmental brain damage has somehow permitted Kim to instantly absorb and then retrieve virtually everything he reads. In addition, he seems to possess two separate, independent optical systems that enable him to read the left page of a book with his left eye while simultaneously reading the right page with his right eye. Normally, however, he uses both eyes together when focusing on hard data and details, or when scanning maps and telephone books.

KimKwip—To his brother, Brian, during a fishing trip: "Bri, why are you feeding the water?"

Showing signs of a rare form of dyslexia, Kim can also read a page that's turned sideways or upside down. But that's not all. A few years ago as we sat in a hotel room one evening, he, without a book in his hand, all at once started chatting about a piece of news. It was then I realized that he can also read mirror images: he was skimming the front page of a newspaper I had inadvertently placed on the mirrored dresser.

Also related to his dyslexia, evidently in the course of his mind's far-flung wanderings he unwittingly transposes the components of his thoughts and expressions. For instance, after arriving home from one of our trips, he commented, "We had a good trip. A little late to be back so soon." Or now and again he'll say something like, "You are here beside me, father. Great I am that you know me." And once he scolded, "Don't just stand there beside yourself!"

While his capacity to reason is somewhat limited, Kim's prodigious memory capabilities have prompted many to label him a genius, blessed with a number of rare gifts. Not only is he a storehouse of everything he's ever read, but to say that he's a fast reader or that he's a voracious reader are absolute understatements. Typically when using both eyes to simultaneously read two ordinary pages, he'll take no more than 15 seconds to scan them, with near total recall. Not long ago during one of our flights, he read Tom Clancy's *The Hunt for Red October* in an hour and 25 minutes. Four months later, when I asked him the name of the book's Russian radio operator, Kim knew it. Then he referred me to the page that described the character and quoted several of its passages.

But why Kim's seeming over-obsession with what some would characterize as "micro-trivia"? What would prompt his weekly 20-plus hours of memorizing details about companies in cities he's never been to? Why would he commit to memory countless names and addresses, area codes and phone numbers and ZIP codes of untold strangers living in towns he'll probably never visit? And why would he spend his remaining waking hours memorizing dates and circumstances surrounding both major and minor world, national, and local events?

Perhaps Kim is engaging in a form of "mental gymnastics," the workings of his mind requiring a certain amount of structure in order to be comfortable; perhaps delving into bare facts is one of his methods of diversion or "brain play"; or perhaps it's his way of feeding the various parts of himself. Or just maybe there is a deeper, more weighty and hidden reason that only he could explain—if only he would or could. Queries into the purposes of his studies usually bring little more than the frustrating reply, "You'll see."

Kim's mind is a peculiar labyrinth, an unsolved mystery, a wonderful interlocking puzzle that may never be entirely and accurately pieced together—at least in this life. It is an enigma, at once a living computer and perpetual calendar. Given a person's date of birth, he can tell her the day of the week she was born, what day of the week her birthday will fall on this year, and what day she'll turn 65 and be able to retire. Likewise, he's able to pinpoint within seconds the date and day of the week for just about any event in history. His brain's collage is made up of hundreds of thousands of details on most any subject, facts he can call up in a moment's notice. It's constantly immersed in a mishmash of thoughts, some of which, unfortunately, confuse him.

Kim is forever feeding his vast mental storage system, his so-called "self-contained internet." However, with so many catalogued items swimming around in his brain, just one little idea can at once send it racing off in countless directions, seeking some sort of connection or symmetry. And out of this figurative "grab bag" of facts and

KimKwip—The tiny girl was covered from head to foot with sticky ice cream, dripping from the triple-decker cone she gripped with both hands. Kim studied her for a moment, then turned to the girl's mother and remarked, "You need to put her back in the freezer before she melts!"

reflections can spring the most profound—or off-the-wall—responses. One local columnist explained Kim's un-single-mindedness this way: "Like an intricate filing system, a mentioned subject will trigger a variety of responses from Kim. He stacks data from commercials, television shows, movies, songs and his book readings into his memory storage. And like a lottery draw, any combination can appear."

Kim's ability to associate one thing with another, seemingly foreign concept—and then yet another—sometimes spooks people. The psychiatrists who interviewed him before *Rain Man* hit the theaters were intrigued and astounded by his range of knowledge *and* how he uses it. They also wanted to know how and where he stores so much information. Several medical centers have since displayed an interest in studying Kim's unique brain structure in an attempt to find out how it manages to generate so many associations so quickly.

After interviewing Kim, neurological experts at Berkeley Medical Research Center in San Francisco were fascinated by his vast knowledge of so many subjects. Because he clearly did not exhibit the standard behavioral patterns of an autistic savant, it was difficult for them to come up with an accurate label for him. So, he was determined to be a "megasavant," with at least 14 major subject areas in which he has extraordinary recall.

The next phase of the research program would have been the injection of radioactive isotopes into Kim's blood stream. As the isotopes circulate through the brain, an MRI scanner traces the wavelengths of the various spectral colors of the isotopes, thus tracing the components of the brain being activated by certain audio cues. In essence, a method of tracking his thought patterns.

It all sounded exciting, especially to the doctors and researchers. But I had to know more about both the scanning techniques and the radioisotopes, so I contacted several doctors and a physicist, and I also talked with Kim's mother, brother, sister, and several close friends to gather their opinions about this next stage of the study.

I learned that, basically, the P.E.T. scanner and the use of radioisotopes are diagnostic procedures to investigate brain-related seizures, Parkinson's disease origins, and similar diseases and activities associated with neurological functions. However, there was a slight chance the radioisotopes could induce complications should there be any type of blockage in the brain. Even though the risk was minimal, we decided to withdraw Kim from the study. It was not a difficult choice after we further explored the negative effects that radioisotopes have been known to produce.

Several months later, the National Institute of Health at Bethesda Research Center contacted us to see if Kim could be a part of their study of "Calendar Calculators." The procedures for their study were, however, identical to those at Berkeley, using radioisotopes, so we had to nix that opportunity as well. Perhaps at some future time those in the medical field will discover an alternative, drug-free way to study the brain's functionings. Maybe then we can unlock the multidimensional door leading to Kim's curious mind-maze. Or maybe it doesn't really matter if we ever find out.

Kim Today

A T THIS WRITING (1996), KIM IS 44 YEARS old, yet he looks as if he is in his mid-thirties. While rather portly, he is in good physical health, though at times he shows marked signs of hyperactivity. His mental condition also appears to be excellent. His emotional state, however, can be rather fragile and volatile, or at least it may appear that way

KimKwip—
Speaking to the Utah State Legislature:
"The work of love is really important..."

to an outsider. Some of his behavioral characteristics include making enginelike noises, as if he is an automobile revving its motor, and he tends to pace back and forth when he gets excited, when the weather turns bad, or when he's disturbed over certain news items he reads, hears on the radio, or sees on television.

His sensitivity to the abuse of others is intense. Frequently, the plights of innocent victims of crime or accident cause him to suffer emotionally—sometimes uncontrollably. He is able to overcome these temporary moments of anxiety with assurances that neither he nor his loved ones are in danger. He responds to love—and, in return, he demonstrates kindness and extols love for everyone.

Even though in the past seven years—following the movie *Rain Man*—his life has been turned upside down, each day Kim's mannerisms are growing more "normal," his personality mushrooming as it emerges from its timid shell. He has grown more engaging, articulate, complex—and capricious—until now he is a rather dynamic person who demands respect and enjoys being different, notions which have become central elements of his heartfelt message to "recognize and respect differences in others."

Unlike the character Raymond Babbitt in *Rain Man*, Kim is not autistic in the usual sense of the word. On the contrary, since his gradual "coming out of the dark" he is remarkably social and compassionate. His repetitious hand movements and his pacing share some similarities with the autism syndrome, but his ability and desire to communicate with others—to initiate dialogue, to share facts, to shake hands and embrace—are essential and noticeable parts of his increasingly exuberant personality.

Kim is totally innocent, totally honest. There are no filters to tell him how to act or to help him sort out what's important from what's not. He has little awareness of humor, except for occasional statements made after-the-fact,

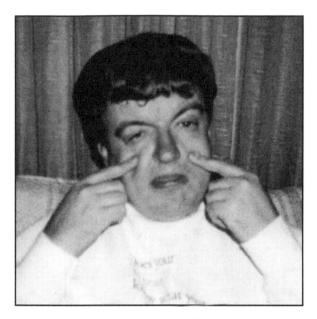

Kim was squinting at the camera, so I told him to open his eyes.
He did, literally, open them, 1996

whereupon he recognizes that his naturally candid remarks sometimes convey a unique sort of wit. He finds it hard to tolerate teasing or joking, largely because he knows how helpless and vulnerable it feels to be made fun of. Hence he is unusually polite and respectful of others.

To Kim, there are no gray areas. Again, like a computer, to him everything is literal. In some ways, Kim is like a three-year-old. He takes words at face value, no questions asked. And he blurts them out with equal ease. Tests show his analytical faculties to be only about 88 percent of normal. And in some ways they're below that figure.

For example, a three-year-old might hear his mom say after a hard day, "I'm pooped!" The child clearly will interpret "I'm pooped!" differently than how the parent intended. Likewise, the three-year-old trying to get past his exhausted mom's feet propped up on the lounger might say, "Mom, can you move your big feet?" Again, the child's not being rude. He's merely comparing his "little" feet to his mother's "big" feet.

Kim outside the home of his favorite author,
Anya Seton Chase, 1973

Like a child, Kim is generally not intimidating—nor can anyone intimidate him. Capable of dominating, orchestrating, and monopolizing a conversation in his eagerness to put across what he is thinking, he sometimes interrupts others, but is practicing how to "wait his turn," immediately backing off when reminded to wait until there is a pause in the conversation. Generally, his social behaviors include courtesy, warmth, and friendliness.

KimKwip—*Speaking to a book club gathering: "Someday I hope to meet [British actor] Sir John Gielgud and [English-born American reporter and television narrator] Alistair Cooke. I have already met and loved Anya Seton Chase. From them my world became."*

Though Kim has little use for material possessions, his love of books is real. I really don't think he could live without the stimulation they provide. One particular scene in the movie *Rain Man* accurately captured Kim's inner

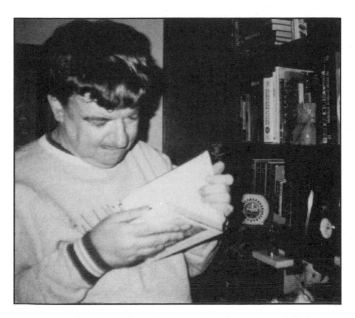

feelings about books. The abducted and confused Raymond, bored at being cooped up in a strange motel, expresses his discomfort in a way that Kim might relate to: "'Course, it's definitely not my room and I don't have my tapioca pudding and the bed's in the wrong place, and that's definitely not my bed . . . 'Course, there're no bookshelves; I'm definitely out of books I . . . I . . . I'm going to be bookless." Kim might react the same way. To be caught "bookless" could be among his worst nightmares.

Second only to Kim's love of books is his love of music. At the mere mention of a musical selection, either classical or contemporary, if he's ever heard the piece he will hum or sing it, in perfect pitch. Plus, being the "generous" person he is, he won't leave it at that. He'll usually go on to recall specifics about the composer's life, other compositions he's written, adaptations of those works, and much more.

KimKwip—Explaining the logic behind his brisk cruise through one particular book: " . . . It had short covers. "

Today, Kim makes friends by the fistful, frequently referring to them by name in an effort to capture their attention so they will listen to what he wants to say. Most people respond positively and interact with him. And with increased exposure, Kim's appropriate participation skills are rapidly improving.

Now that we've been challenged to share Kim's message and unique abilities with the world, we spend about half our time visiting cities big and small, where hundreds of people a week are meeting "Rain Man" for the first time. He's a little more hyperactive when we're on the road. In a hotel, Kim often can be found pacing along a bare wall gripping one of his many coiled "dirty belts" (a 12-inch piece of venetian blind cord with knots at each end that he always carries with him—so named because after a day's use it becomes quite soiled) and staring at it as he twists and twirls it between his thumbs and index fingers. He'll also reminisce with me for hours, opening conversations with "Remember the time . . . ?" and "Remember when . . . ?"

KimKwip—To the curator of a historical museum in Omaha: "You need to fix the sign in your parking lot. It says the trouble took place on Wednesday, August 11, 1842. August 11th that year landed on a Thursday."

He seems never to tire. All the new experiences he's having, they're so fun and fulfilling to him. In fact, I often remind him that the day he gets bored or grows weary of the daily grind, of being "Rain Man" and meeting people, that's the day we'll quit.

The other day I received a letter from a man who had met Kim for the first time just a month or so before. In it he described the experience from his perspective:

> The second he came through the door **he** was in charge. He couldn't dress himself this morning, but he was in charge now. He announced himself as "Rain Man" (between the other topics he was discussing all at once) and sat on a chair near the corner. We asked him to join us at

the table where we had soft drinks. Kim immediately rose and moved in our direction, still addressing multiple subjects. He extended his hand without even slowing down. It was the limp, quick handshake of a two-year-old with a new skill. Then he sat down and started in on some new topics, while simultaneously keeping some of the old ones going. It was amazing. You name a subject and his mind steers the discussion onto any of a dozen different avenues of thought, which can then lead into a song, a quote, any bit of information.

Immediately I liked him. He has the simple honesty of a child yet knowledge much beyond a clear-minded 90-year-old. The most surprising thing is how happy and personable and confident he is. This is no doubt a tribute to his family, particularly his father, who trails along behind like a parent at the playground, watching his son explore and learn. And yet he knows there is something special here. More than his son becoming a doctor or a lawyer, "Rain Man" is unique—completely, delightfully unique.

Unfortunately, his words cannot nearly keep up with the host of thoughts, stories, and subjects going around in his single-hemisphere, megasavant head. Apparently the ideas are coming too fast and from too many directions for him to deal with all at once . . .

In many ways Kim is a normal, healthy, forty-something man. He loves sports, television, and current events. But his real love is knowledge; he wants to know everything. He wants to know the address and phone number of people he . . .will never meet. Memorizing phone books is fun—a sport.

He is not held back by the concept of "What are you ever going to **do** with all of this knowledge?" . . . He wants to know things because he **can** know them. He remembers; he recalls. And with knowledge comes potential.

Talking with him, it may seem as if his mind has wandered, that he's not keeping up with the conversation. But then he'll say something that lets you know he is still very much in tune with what's going on around him.

Maybe he's just bored, his mind wanting to scoot on ahead to another topic.

...A simple connection may elude him one minute, while he deals well with a complex strand of logic the next. Problem-solving seems more like a place he stumbles upon rather than a destination he sets out for. But when your mind is going that fast, I guess you cover a lot of ground... Sometimes he even repeats a remark over and over, not quite aware that he has already shared it once.

Much of his life is out of his control; but so is ours. It doesn't seem as if he starts with a problem and then seeks a solution. He starts with the answers to a million problems, and then works backwards...

Perhaps becoming acquainted with Kim will offer hope and solace to parents bearing the singular burdens and blessings of caring for "backward" youngsters—that they will know that they're not alone. For that matter, I'm convinced that all of us, living in a fragile world filled with toxins and high-speed collisions and such, have undergone "brain damage" of some sort or another. And I am equally convinced that each of us is endowed with some degree of "savantism." I guess the question is do we really know ourselves? Are we able to focus on and cultivate our own unique talents? As parents, are we nurturing to the best of our ability the inner, God-given genius of each of our children? And do we recognize the vast, untapped potential that lies within each person we meet?

An unidentified soul once reminded us: "Be kind. Remember, everyone you meet is fighting a hard battle." Kim, like all of us, is fighting—and, for the most part, winning—his daily battles. He at once entertains, educates, and moves his listeners, urging them not to make fun of those with lower than normal mental capacity and to understand that everyone is entitled to be treated as they themselves would want to be treated. It is his hope that his step–by–step rise in confidence and self-worth will teach a greater tolerance and respect for others, regardless of ability or disability.

My hope is that Kim's story will lift siblings and other family members of those who are "different," not only to a better understanding of their son or daughter, brother or sister, but to a higher perception of themselves and to a better sense of how to approach relationships in general. That those who come to know and appreciate Kim might come to better appreciate their own loved ones.

To everyone he boldly yet lovingly takes his message: "Recognize and respect differences in others. Then, treat them as you want them to treat you so we can have the kind of world we want to live in. Care and share. Be your best!"

A single word identifies this man, my son: *remarkable*.

Still, as remarkable as he is, in my mind he would have remained forever isolated in the shadowy fringes of life had it not been for several giving people, people whom we now consider among our dearest friends.

In 1979, my wife and I separated. Then when we divorced in 1981, Kim started traveling with me. And though he opted to remain camouflaged in the background, at least he was forced to observe the basic courtesies of meeting and being around people.

Then in 1984, in an amazing turn of fate, Kim and I came into contact with screenwriter Barry Morrow, a wonderfully talented and caring man who, showing an immediate interest in Kim, took him aside for a few hours to probe the inner workings of his mind. Afterwards he offered to write a story based on Kim's amazing abilities. We accepted the gracious offer.

The change in Kim since *Rain Man* has been striking. The post-movie Kim has matured tremendously. His mask of isolation and loneliness steadily faded away. Where before he would never call attention to himself in the slightest, now he's comfortable with who he is and how he fits into other people's lives. He knows who he is and what he's capable of doing. Friends who haven't seen Kim for several years say they can't believe the incredible progress he's made. He's come so far—as a person.

PART II

KIM'S "COMING OUT"— THE JOURNEY BEGINS

The Way to Make an Instant Impression and a Lifelong Friend

IT ALL STARTED IN ARLINGTON, TEXAS. IN 1984, AT THE headquarters of the National Association for Retarded Citizens ("The Arc"), I was serving as chair of the organization's Communications Committee. A motley volunteer group of advertising, marketing, public relations, and writing professionals, we were trying to increase nationwide awareness of The Arc and its local chapters through media public service announcements and other marketing vehicles.

Barry Morrow, one of the most talented, personable and caring individuals I have ever met, had been invited by The Arc's Director of Communications, Liz Moore, to assist on our committee. A prominent screenwriter who a few years earlier had been honored with two of television's prestigious Emmy awards for writing the chronicle *Bill* and its sequel, *Bill II* (starring Mickey Rooney as a college coffee shop manager who is retarded and who touches the hearts of a circle of university students), Morrow had accepted the invitation.

On this particular trip, Kim had come with me to

Arlington. When I am to be away more than a couple of days, it is a bit awkward for anyone else to attend to his grooming needs. Besides, he's really a lot of fun when we're traveling and sight-seeing. He already knows nearly everything there is to know about the cities we visit.

Barry came into the meeting about 9:00 A.M. and I introduced him to Kim. Kim, normally a recluse in such settings, came close, looked Barry square in the eyes and said, "Barry Morrow, think about yourself!"

Barry, stunned, just stood there for a moment. Then he turned to me and said, "Wow! That's some greeting! May I take him out in the hallway for a few minutes?"

Several hours later they returned, and Barry asked, "Where'd you get this guy?"

"What do you mean?" I asked.

"Well," Barry explained, "we went over to the computer center and corrected some of the ZIP codes on the membership lists. Then we went into the library and Kim knew just about every author and every book on the shelves."

But that wasn't all that had impressed Barry. "Next," he continued, "we talked about baseball. You know, I'm a member of a baseball club in Los Angeles, and I figure I have a pretty good knowledge of the game. Well, now I know someone who knows a lot more about it than I ever will.

"Then, after discussing a little football, basketball, boxing, and even horse racing, Kim went on to tell me what roads I should take on my way back to Claremont, California, where I live. He told me what cities I'd pass through, their area and ZIP codes, plus, just for the helluvit, he told me my phone number and some facts about Claremont."

By now Barry's enthusiasm was overflowing. "I also told him my date of birth and he gave me the day of the week I was born, the day of the week this year, and the day of the week and year I would turn 65 so I could think about retiring. We also discussed events of the Revolutionary War, the Civil War, World Wars I and II, Korea, and Vietnam. No way could one person know that much. No way!"

Barry then looked me in the eye and his voice took on a serious tone. I had no way of knowing at the time, but those next few minutes were to be a turning point in our lives. "You know, Fran, I want to write a story about Kim."

A story about Kim? I pondered the significance of his proposal. Of course I knew it was a real tribute, but maybe, I wondered, he's just being courteous. After all, we had just met that morning . . .

Two years later, in the fall of 1986, Barry phoned from Los Angeles to tell us the exciting news: United Artists/Metro Goldwyn Mayer had just purchased his script about Kim, tentatively titled *Rain Man.*

This was to be the first step in Kim's eventual "coming out" and into a new life for both of us, where every day is challenging and fascinating.

As Kim so often says, "When it rains . . . share your umbrella." Barry Morrow included us under his wide-open umbrella! His insights helped salvage Kim's life. And they were also a much-needed source of light in making my own life whole again.

A Special Day with Dustin

M R. HOFFMAN WOULD LIKE TO MEET YOU AND KIM AT your convenience." The distinctively New York-flavored voice on the other end of the line continued. "He would like to visit Kim at your home in Salt Lake sometime in January. Could you phone me back with some possible dates?"

"I'll check Kim's schedule and get right back to you," I replied.

It had been only days since Barry's call, and already Dustin Hoffman's New York office was phoning to confirm that he wanted to play the lead role. That would wrap up the deal: *Rain Man* was on its way!

After looking over our calendar, I returned the call and gave the secretary several dates that would work out for us. They would get back to us, she said.

About a week passed with no response. Tomorrow, I thought, I would call again; by then Kim's 24-hour-a-day obsession with the possibility of meeting Dustin Hoffman had become for me a 24-hour-a-day frustration. But when we arrived home late that evening, the message machine was blinking and the first call was from Dustin's New York agency.

> *KimKwip—Watching several tiny ants gathering pieces of bread crumbs and carrying them into a crack in our patio's cement: "How do you suppose they make their TV dinners?"*

"Mr. Hoffman has been detained in Europe," was the disappointing word I got from his secretary when I called back the next morning. "But," she added, "he would like to visit with you in Hollywood on February 6th at 8 A.M. He's sorry for having to miss meeting Kim in your home, but his schedule isn't always predictable."

As she went on reciting the details of our upcoming trip, I sat in a fog—a veritable dreamland: " . . . leave February 5th . . . first-class tickets at the United Airlines check-in counter three days before the flight . . . Los Angeles Airport . . . reservations provided for the Century Plaza Hotel in Beverly Hills . . . "

Finally, my mind clicked back into gear. "We've also talked with Barry Morrow, and he plans to meet you at the airport," the secretary announced. "Barry will call you to verify times and places and such. Mr. Hoffman is very excited to visit with Kim."

The next several days were anxious ones for both of us. We pulled our clothes out of the closet and selected which of them to pack. In a rare display of "cramming," Kim spent a couple of hours reviewing the maps of Los Angeles and its surrounding cities.

We arrived at the airport about an hour before departure and picked up our tickets. We decided to carry our baggage on the plane with us so as to not risk having it end up in Hawaii.

Thinking back now, our stroll down the terminal to the boarding gate was reminiscent of the poster that introduced *Rain Man* in the movie theaters and magazines: Dustin and Tom walking down the roadway leading from Wallbrook—the institution where Raymond (Rain Man) had spent most of his life—two men, one out to seize a portion of his inheritance, who instead unwittingly overcomes his "handicaps" in the areas of kindness and understanding; the other, the "kidnapped" and agitated Raymond.

But our walk was different! We were gamely striding towards a new world, one entirely unknown to Kim—and, for that matter, not too familiar to me, either. The sunrises ahead of us would be filled with new horizons, meeting hundreds of thousands of new people, making new friends, visiting new places. And Kim would mature and flourish in ways not thought possible.

As we boarded the plane and took our seats in the first-class section right behind the plane's door, a flight attendant standing alongside the copilot stopped to talk with us. "We understand you're going to Hollywood to see Dustin Hoffman."

"And we shall do that!" trumpeted Kim, rolling his head back, his eyes glistening and his lips spread in a full grin. "We meet Barry in a couple of hours. Then we're going to the Warner Lot to meet the people at United Artists."

"How did you know we were meeting with Dustin Hoffman?" I asked.

The attendant smiled. "We've been waiting since two days ago when we received the letter confirming your reservations from his agency. The letter included some special instructions for us."

"What is your birth date?" Kim asked.

"My birth date?" replied the stewardess.

"Yes," I invited, "month, day, and year." She told Kim and he immediately spouted out the day she was born, what day of the week her birthday was that year, and the day and year she would turn 65.

"Amazing!" She motioned to the copilot. "Tell him your birthday." He did—and about ten seconds later the copilot knew all about his calendar history, too.

"Without telling Kim what state a small city is in that you are familiar with, tell him only the name of the city and he will locate it for you," I added.

"How about Terre Haute?" quizzed the stewardess.

"It's in Indiana on highways 70 and 41," Kim began. "North is Fountain and Linton, and south is Vincennes. You are served by GTE North, area code 812. Thank you."

"And, if she were home this weekend, what TV stations would she be able to watch?" I asked.

"Two regions. Central Indiana and Eastern Illinois. You know, Sony's recording facilities are there," Kim answered.

Both of them seemed awed by his remarks. "How does he know all this?" asked the flight attendant.

I shrugged my shoulders. "We wish we knew. So do the people who have been testing him on and off the past few months. No one really knows. He just seems not to be able to forget anything he reads or hears. Since early childhood."

After describing Kim's rare condition, how he differs socially and emotionally from most identified "autistic" savants, and how he has become somewhat of an authority in some 14 or 15 subject areas, I was met with a stream of questions.

"What are some of his favorite topics?"

"World history, American history, any state's history. I guess most countries' histories as well. Classical music and its composers. He can hum most of the selections ever written.

Literature and authors. Geography—worldwide. Professional and major college sports—baseball, football, basketball . . . All about the space program. Some Shakespeare. All the stories included in the *Reader's Digest* condensed volumes for the past 30 or so years. Religions—books in the Old and New Testaments; Mormon books and history. Those kinds of subjects.

"The only areas he doesn't like to talk about are abstract mathematics, chemistry, and physics, since he isn't fond of studying them. And he's not a fan of trivia found in *The Guinness Book of Records*. He's really a very intellectual person."

During the flight to Los Angeles, each member of the flight crew stopped by to ask Kim one thing or another. Mostly birthdays—often their spouses' or children's. A couple on the plane threw out some questions about football teams and players. Kim answered them all.

As we made our way off the plane, Barry was there to greet us, vibrant as ever. When he spotted us, he bounded across the floor, threw his arms around Kim, and expressed how happy he was to see us. "You're still that good man, Barry Morrow," blared Kim. Then, as if to preserve the intensity of the moment, he looked around and asked, "Where do we go from here?"

Barry seemed to enjoy Kim's obvious excitement. "It's only about 11:00. I thought we might drive into downtown L.A. and have lunch at one of my favorite restaurants."

"Where's that?" Kim asked.

"Downtown. They have super chicken potpies. You like potpies, Kim?"

> *KimKwip—Kim is seldom wrong. During a tour of the SAC Museum in Omaha, a plaque caught his attention: "LeMay wasn't made an Air Force lieutenant general until 1943. That picture says it was in 1942."*

"Love 'em. Dad fixes them for me sometimes when he goes out to dinner with Mary Ruth."

Barry knew how to keep Kim occupied. "And how is Mary

Ruth—with the gold tooth?"

"She's really good, Barry. Still has that gold tooth," he cackled, placing his finger against Barry's lips and adding, "And I will always remember that day when you came to Snowbird and she picked you up at the airport and you hugged her and said, 'You must be Mary Ruth with the gold tooth!'"

Barry's grin widened. "I remember that day, too, Kim! And, remember, we all drove around Salt Lake and you showed me a lot of interesting sites."

"Yes, I remember. And now, Barry Morrow, we're in Los Angeles. To get to downtown, you need to take the airport exit onto La Cienga Boulevard, don't you?"

"Right . . . we'll take La Cienga as far as . . . "

"To Hollywood and Sunset . . . " Kim interrupted.

"And," Barry broke back in, pleased to play Kim's game, "then you go up Sunset and the restaurant is right near Mann's Chinese Theater." He turned to me. "You've been to Los Angeles a few times before?"

"Once before, back in 1965," I said, "but he knows all the main roads, the freeway exits, most of the downtown streets, and nearly all the locations of businesses, movie houses, ball parks. He also knows a lot of history about Los Angeles. California, too. He'll probably make comments as you drive along. But," I warned, "don't be unnerved if he flips back and forth from subject to subject."

Needless to say, our ride into town was an interesting one. Kim knew every street and would advise Barry every few blocks as to what intersections were coming up, how far it was to the exit we were looking for, and what buildings we would pass along the way.

A few minutes into the drive, Barry leaned over to me. "You know, Fran, I still can't believe this! What about other cities? Has he memorized all their streets and addresses, too?"

"Ask him about your hometown," I suggested.

Barry Morrow and Kim, trying on one another's glasses, 1989

Barry glanced over at Kim, who by now was staring at his fingers, which were vigorously moving back and forth in front of his face. "What do you see when you look at your fingers like that, Kim?" asked Barry.

"Lots of things you wonder about, Barry Morrow," Kim answered, seemingly oblivious to our surroundings. Then, "Just four more exits," he blurted out, his eyes still mesmerized by the blur of his fingers. "Then you go off into chicken potpie land!"

Finally maneuvering into the rear of "chicken potpie land's" filled parking lot, we strolled down the sidewalk to the front door. The place was packed.

"My, Barry. Lots of Californians like chicken potpies," quipped Kim.

"This is a very popular spot, Kim," Barry nodded.

Before long, our host escorted us to a small table in the center of the room and asked, "Will this be OK?" There weren't any empty booths, so we settled down at the table, seating Kim next to the unoccupied chair so he could stretch out his left arm as he ate. Barry's mouth turned up slightly. "So, Kim's a lefty?"

"Yes," I smiled, "only one in the family."

After a marvelous lunch, we sauntered back out to the car, and Barry steered us out into traffic. He was faithfully following Kim's directions for how to get to the Century Plaza Hotel, but then Barry came up with another idea. "Before we check in, let's go see a couple of special places!"

"What places?" asked Kim.

Barry, still captivated by Kim's innocent enthusiasm, motioned left. "Just a couple of blocks away is the Sidewalk of the Stars and Mann's Chinese Theater. Lots of fun posters and other things to see there!"

We pulled into the parking lot behind the theater. Slowly moving along the sidewalk, reading the names of stars, we came to the famous Mann's. Everything was closed except for a small photo shop tucked away behind several large poster displays of famous films that had played there when it was known as "Graumann's."

KimKwip—
Commenting on a small girl walking alongside her bicycle: "Maybe her bicycle ran out of gas."

Barry put his arm around Kim and led him toward the photo shop. "Let's have our picture taken." He introduced the three of us to the fellow in the shop. Then we stepped onto the small, draped, boothlike platform.

"What kind of a camera is that?" asked Barry.

"It's a lot like a computer scanner," replied the photographer. "The photo's scanned onto the paper in a series of fine, horizontal lines." He pulled a couple of samples off the table and held them up. "This will be a great souvenir, Kim!" Barry remarked as he positioned himself on Kim's left and wrapped his right arm around his shoulder.

"Sure will," I responded, shifting over to Kim's right.

We said "cheese," the camera hummed, and within minutes there was the picture. An unusual, but nice picture.

"How much to put the photo on a T-shirt?" Barry asked as he fingered the sleeve of a picture-printed shirt hanging near the photographer's desk.

"Eight bucks."

"Let's get you back in front of the camera, Kim," Barry insisted. "We'll put your picture on a T-shirt and give it to Dustin in the morning, OK? And how about a warmup shirt for me?"

No sooner said, than a larger-than-life picture of Kim printed in dark blue appeared on a white shirt with black trim. "Dustin will know he's the real Rain Man when we give him this, won't he?" Kim grinned.

Arriving at the hotel, we waved off the doorman and the bellhop and carried our luggage over to the registration desk. "Rain Man is here!" announced Kim. By now he was almost euphoric.

"Yes, we've been expecting you," smiled the desk clerk.

"We'll only be here tonight," Kim gushed. "Going to meet with Dustin in the morning."

Our room was magnificent. It had everything—two showers, robes, a stocked bar. The bathroom alone was nearly as large as our living room at home. And what's more the 22nd-floor balcony provided the perfect perch for checking out the sights. Kim pointed out a number of buildings he'd read about, told us what they were used for and when they were built.

Barry interrupted our rubbernecking. "While you unpack, I have a couple of errands to take care of. I want to talk to some people over at one of the movie lots who want to meet Kim. "Oh," he turned back to us, "the guys who run United Artists/MGM want us to meet with the whole staff for a few minutes tomorrow after our session with Dustin, or the morning after if time runs out." Then he added as he waved and departed, "I'll be back about six o'clock, out in front, and we'll go to dinner."

We were left alone, in that quiet, spacious room. "Stretch out for a bit, Kim," I said, "while I get our clothes out of the bags. OK?"

He eased down onto one of the smooth beds. "Rest is important, Dad. Big day tomorrow. I'll have to ask Dustin about a couple of scenes in *Kramer versus Kramer* that got him his 1980 Oscar. Remember, Dad? It won five big ones: Best Picture, Best Actor, Best Supporting Actress—Meryl Streep—Best Director, and Best Adapted Screenplay."

"Know who directed *Kramer versus Kramer?*" I asked, more out of habit than curiosity.

"Robert Benton, a Stanley Jaffe production," Kim remarked absently.

"Yes, I'm sure the two of you will have a lot to talk about."

After thumbing through several large phone directories and a couple of brochures in the room, Kim rolled over, facing me. "Dad," he asked, his usual placid face taking on a slightly puzzled expression, "would this ever have happened to you if I hadn't been born?"

"No, never," I answered solemnly. "This is a special thing that is happening to a special person."

Kim exhaled, apparently soothed by my answer. And two minutes later he was snoring. His hands were extended upward, covering his ears, but the peacefulness evident in his breathing told me that here was one happy guy. It's not always easy to tell when Kim is enjoying himself, but this time there was no question about it.

After a fine rest and an even better dinner, Barry dropped us off at the hotel, as he still had a long drive to Claremont. We planned to be out in front of the hotel early the next morning to keep our 8:30 appointment with Dustin at the studio.

I staggered out of bed at about six o'clock. It had been a fairly tough night for me, but Kim had been down a solid seven hours. After we had shaved and showered, I helped him dress. Not surprisingly, his mind was racing wildly, trying to balance a thousand different thoughts at once, from meeting with Dustin to contemplating the plots from various movies, plays, and operas.

At breakfast in the hotel coffee shop, several waiters stopped to ask about the day they were born and the day they could begin collecting Social Security. Several shared the towns they grew up in, or had lived in, and Kim described their locations, their TV stations and area codes. If a town was located in a historical area of the eastern United States, he would recount some important event or Revolutionary/Civil War battle that had taken place there or nearby. One young man wasn't aware that Joe Namath had been born in Beaver Falls, Pennsylvania, a small town just south of where he had been raised.

On our way out of the hotel to meet Barry, Kim spoke with the doorman and discovered that he had played football for the Los Angeles Rams but had retired the same year Merlin Olsen joined the team. However, since Merlin is one of Kim's favorite people and athletes—and the doorman admitted that he had played with him in spring practice—Kim just had to tell him about Merlin's years at Utah State University in Logan, Utah, his days with the Rams, and several things about his family and career. The doorman shook his head. "How does he know these things?"

"I wish I could explain it," I replied. "He reads everything, every atlas, almanac, book, magazine. If it's been printed, he's probably read it."

"Every day," I added, "he spends at least three hours reading, learning, storing—waiting to recall whatever he needs to in order to express himself. I guess you can't totally accept these things about Kim unless you spend quite a bit of time with him. Even then the amazing things he's able to do sometimes still seem impossible. He's unreal!"

I beamed with pride as the doorman surveyed Kim, who by then seemed oblivious to our conversation, his eyes focused on his fingers. "Someday, I hope you, your family, and all your friends get to meet Kim. I wish every person on this earth could talk with him. It would be a better place for everyone."

Barry's car circled into the hotel loading zone. He leaped from the car almost before it stopped. "Well, guys, are you ready for the big event?"

"I'm ready as I shall be," Kim's voice boomed. "We are about ten minutes away from the studio, aren't we?"

"Yep! About ten minutes," Barry responded, his eyes rolling upward.

Barry parked in the rear of the studio and we helped Kim out of the front seat, locked the doors, and hurried to the reception area. "And you must be Kim?" greeted the pleasant woman behind the desk. "Mr. Hoffman is two doors down the hall and to your left."

"Thanks," said Barry. "We're just a little nervous, you know."

"Not me, Barry," Kim chimed in. "Let's go find Dustin before he meets me." Kim's bold yet jumbled remark and his burning enthusiasm—although I could sense how jittery he was—greatly eased our fears.

When we knocked on the door, a bearded, gray-haired man opened it. "You don't look like Dustin," said Kim.

"I'm Murray Schisgal," said the man, gesturing for us to come in.

Kim hardly missed a beat: "You wrote *Tootsie.* Jessica Lange got the 1982 Academy Award for Best Supporting Actress. Produced and directed by Sydney Pollack; he's a friend of our friend, Robert Redford, who lives just south of us at Sundance Ski Resort. I once helped William DeVane with his horses near Redford's place."

"Yes, that's right," Murray stammered, appearing amused and amazed at the same time.

"Fine film. Dustin deserved an Oscar for that one, too!" Kim enthused.

Just then a rather small, unassuming man, wearing a denim jacket, canvas shoes, and Levi's, arrived at the door and approached us. Kim reached out, put his hands on the man's shoulders, pressed his nose to the man's nose and said solemnly, "Dustin Hoffman, from this moment on we shall be as one."

Hoffman turned to me. "Did you tell him to say that?"

I shook my head. "No. I guess he's been thinking a lot about this special moment."

Dustin shook hands with Barry and me and escorted us all into the room. "Just take a seat on the sofa," he motioned, flashing us a friendly grin. "I've got a couple of phone calls to make, then I'll be right with you."

"Dustin," Kim chimed in, as if Dustin's agenda would just have to wait. "I've got a present for you!"

Dustin, yielding to the gentle, childlike urgency in Kim's eyes and voice, moved forward, his hands outstretched to receive the small sack Kim held out. Folding back the tightly creased paper, he withdrew the photo-printed T-shirt we had made at Mann's Theater and unfurled it for all to see. Everyone clapped and told Kim how great it looked.

Next Dustin took off his jacket and laid it across a chair, stripped off his shirt, and wiggled into his new Rain Man T-shirt. "How do I look, Kim?"

"You look just like me!" Kim laughed, pacing and grinning in nervous excitement.

Dustin let out a chuckle, then walked to the corner of the room and began dialing the phone. Meanwhile, a tall, bearded man in his early thirties approached Kim. "Hello, Kim. I'm Marty Brest."

"You did a fine job directing *Beverly Hills Cop*," Kim said.

"Thank you. I'm happy to meet you. I've also been selected to direct *Rain Man*."

Kim's eyes brightened anew. "We'll get to work together a lot, won't we?"

"I hope so," said Marty. Then, ushering forward another, shorter gentleman, he added, "And this is Roger Bierbaum. He'll be working on the movie, too."

"Thanks, Roger, for being Barry's friend," said Kim, sidling over and extending his hand.

Roger took Kim's hand and gave it a firm shake. "Pretty strong," he nodded. "You must spend a lot of time at Muscle Beach"—a remark which drew laughter from everyone in the room.

"Hey, Kim," Dustin called out, holding his hand over the mouthpiece of the phone. "I'm talking to my wife in New York."

"Your first or second wife?"

"My *only* wife," Dustin answered emphatically. "And she was born on June 17, 1941."

"That was a Tuesday," Kim spouted, "this year she will turn 46 on a Wednesday, and if she has to go back to work, she will be able to retire in 2006 on a Saturday."

Dustin's eyes widened. "Wow! How does he do that so fast?"

"Maybe someday we'll find out," I offered. "He won't—or can't—share his computation methods with anyone."

Dustin, who had scribbled Kim's dates on a scratch pad, withdrew his hand from the receiver and shared with his wife the birthday information. "Kim," said Dustin moments later, "my wife is going to write down our children's dates of birth. If I call her back in a few minutes, can you calculate the days of the week for her?"

Kim smiled at the prospect. "I'd like to meet Mrs. Hoffman. She must be a good lady to have a man like you around the house."

"Nicely said," returned Dustin. He hung up the phone and walked over to join us.

"Well, Kim, it's a real pleasure to meet you," Dustin said, formally matching Kim's sincere disposition. "I've heard a little about you. I understand you like to read."

"Reading is what it's all about. Thank you," said Kim, a gleam in his eye.

"And being able to remember almost all of it makes it even better," Barry interjected.

Hoffman waved his hand toward the others in the room. "You've met these gentlemen?"

"All of them. Past and present," Kim answered.

Dustin's smile widened; he'd already glanced over at me several times during his chat with Kim. "And you're Fran, Kim's father? I've tried to phone you several times, but we both seem to have pretty busy schedules."

"It's an unusual time for us," I replied, patting Kim's arm. "For the past several months, neuropsychiatrists in Salt Lake have taken an interest in Kim's savant abilities. They want to probe his brain and uncanny memory. We've been meeting with quite a few medical people."

"And what's their conclusion?"

"Mostly they're astonished, mystified. They haven't seen anyone like him before. So-called 'idiot savants' have been identified through the years. But according to the limited research available, they have all been 'autistic savants.' Kim may be one of a kind, so they say."

Intrigued, Dustin turned to Kim. "I understand you know quite a bit about history, Kim—all kinds of history. Can you tell me about the Battle of Bunker Hill?"

Kim looked at Dustin. "Took place in Charlestown on Breed's Hill, near Boston, on June 17, 1775, between the Americans and the British."

I fished for further information: "Do you know the day of the week it was fought?"

"It was a Saturday," he replied.

Engrossed by what he was seeing and hearing, Dustin abruptly changed the subject. "In 1836, do you know who was president of the United States?"

"James K. Polk was president. He was born in North Carolina in 1795 and died in Tennessee in 1849. His vice president was George Dallas."

"Do you know where he was born?"

"In Pennsylvania."

"I understand you don't like to do math problems," Dustin noted.

"I get enough math in my job," answered Kim flatly.

"He helps with the payroll for about 150 handicapped workers at the sheltered workshop where he works," I explained, "the Columbus Community Center in Salt Lake. He figures each person's daily production earnings—they're paid by-the-piece, mostly assembly work. Then he computes the gross and net amounts of each check so they can be made

At work sorting checks, 1996

out. Does it in his head without using an adding machine or calculator. He also helps distribute the checks."

Dustin squinted, then turned his attention back to Kim. "If I asked you what 320 times 160 was, could you tell me?"

"You double the top number, halve the bottom number, double the top, halve the bottom, double the top, halve the bottom, double the top, halve the bottom and then multiply the top number, 5120, by the bottom number, 10, and you have 51,200. But I don't do math problems," Kim concluded with a nod of finality. "Thank you!"

"Just like that!" said Dustin, a flabbergasted expression spreading across his face.

"Just like that, thank you," repeated Kim.

As Kim paced back and forth along a bare wall in the room, tugging on his length of blind cord, Dustin asked me, "Do you have an extra cord like the one Kim's using?"

"Here." I withdrew a dirty belt from my pants pocket and placed it in his hand. "I always carry a few spares. They get lost or worn out after awhile. It's Kim's security blanket. Every now and then, he'll hold it in front of his face and twist the hell out of it—like right now." I pointed in Kim's direction. "They get so threadbare that I have to go to the hardware store and buy another fifty feet about every other month."

Hoffman took the cord, knots on each end, and sauntered towards Kim. Kim didn't pay any attention to his advance. Then, for most of an hour, Dustin duplicated every motion Kim made—including the cord twisting—following him around like a second skin and asking him questions. On occasion, Kim would turn his head to watch Dustin's impersonations, but did nothing about it.

Others in the room kept Kim busy asking him questions about British monarchs, the Bible, baseball, horse racing, dates, times and places... When one of them inquired about Puccini, Kim hummed aloud a couple of the composer's most famous compositions, coupling his melodies with facts: "You know, Puccini was born in Lucca, Italy, on December 22, 1858, and died in Brussels on November 12, 1924. His most popular operas are *La Boheme* and *Madame Butterfly*." Kim then proceeded to hum a few bars from each.

While Kim meandered about the room, the actor maintained his shadowing routine, angling around his subject in a sort of dance. Actually, he wasn't really mimicking him: he was trying to mirror and implant in himself some of Kim's basic behavioral patterns, so later he could incorporate them into his Raymond character.

At lunch break, I took Kim to the rest room. A sign posted on the door said "CLOSED." One of the nearby production staff members directed us to another rest room on the other side of the building. When we approached it, however, we also found a sign on its door reading "COLOR EMPLOYEES ONLY."

That got Kim's dander up. "Haven't they heard about the Civil Rights Act?" he babbled to himself. A fellow just exiting the door explained the sign. "You're in the production area where the movie *Color* is being produced. Go ahead and use the rest room. It's OK."

After I had reassembled Kim's clothes and helped him wash and dry his hands, Dustin and several others came through the door. "Wait in the hall for us," he said, smiling. "I want you to say hi to an old friend of mine."

When Dustin emerged, we made our way down the hall, where Dustin knocked on a door bearing the nameplate "Dennis Hopper." This sent Kim launching into the theme from the movie *Easy Rider*. His croonings echoed down the hall:

> *Get your motor runnin',*
> *Head out on the highway . . .*

Without a second's thought, Dustin joined in and pushed the door open just as Hopper was about to turn the handle:

> *Lookin' for adventure*

And whatever comes my way . . .

Then, in one of the most out-of-the-ordinary scenes I have ever witnessed, Hopper, too, joined in, momentarily strumming an imaginary guitar, then putting his arm around Dustin's shoulder as Dustin draped his arm around Kim's waist, and, over and over, like a trio of uninhibited drunks, their uneven voices belted out the familiar refrain:

Born to be wiiild!

Born to be wiiild!

Finally ending their serenade, Dustin, breathing somewhat heavily, motioned toward Kim. "Dennis, meet Kim—the *real* Rain Man!"

Taking Kim's hand, Hopper said, "Pleased to meet you, Kim. How did you know the lyrics from *Easy Rider?*"

"My brother Brian and my sister Ali used to play it on our record player," Kim chuckled, remembering. "And I read a lot of things about it."

"Such as?" invited Dustin.

Kim innocently yet happily took up the challenge. "Jack Nicholson and Peter Fonda and Dennis. Exciting movie. Came out in 1970."

"And, Dennis," Dustin interjected, "when were you born?"

"When was I born?" Hopper tilted his head to the right.

"Month, day, and year," Dustin urged impatiently.

"February 18, 1936."

"You are a year older than Dustin," Kim began. "You're 51." Then he added, "But you look much younger than Dustin."

Dustin's pupils at once went down to the floor; his chin followed. He shook his head a couple of times. Then, straightening up, he cast his eyes around the group, lifted an amused eyebrow, and pursed his lips to stifle a grin.

"Dennis," Kim went on, unperturbed, "you were born on a Tuesday and this year it'll fall on a Wednesday. You can retire when you turn 65 in 2001 on a Sunday." Kim then began humming the theme from the movie *2001, A Space Odyssey*, ending with a hearty, "Thank you!"

"Thank *you*, Kim!" said Dustin.

"How does he do that?" asked Dennis, crinkling up his nose.

"No one seems to know," Dustin shrugged, "but then, telling people about their birthdays is really insignificant, comparatively. You ought to hear some of the other things he can do."

"Like?" Dennis asked.

"Like," Dustin pounced on the question, "any kind of historical information from any time in any country, the Bible, professional sports, movies, actors and actresses, geography, telephone book information, the space program, authors and literature—especially Shakespeare. Just don't ask him anything about math. I did, and he made a fool of me."

After strolling from the building into the sunshine to take a few pictures and catch a breath of fresh air, we returned to the studio for another question-and-answer session. Dustin again peppered some questions at Kim, who, still considerably nervous at having been placed in such a spotlight, every few minutes scrambled from his seat to pace the room.

At last Dustin asked, "Kim, do you believe in God?"

Kim's response was hauntingly poignant: "In God there is mystery. In my heart there is mystery. Two mysteries make one belief. To know oneself is to know God. Thank you."

The room fell silent, everyone's eyes on Kim. Then Dustin turned and asked, "Is he religious?"

"He has never been baptized into any church," I explained. "One of his excuses is that he never learned to swim. You see, The Church of Jesus Christ of Latter-day Saints, the Mormons, baptize by immersion. My parents were converts to the LDS Church from England."

Dustin grinned and repeated, "Didn't learn how to swim! Have the Mormons since changed the process?"

"No. We believe that because of Kim's innocent, childlike nature he doesn't require baptism. But for some twenty years he's attended Mormon seminary held five days weekly at his sheltered workshop; he graduated 20 times—has 20 diplomas. Because of his reasoning limitations, I think his religion is what he's read and heard, not what he contemplates and tries to reason about. He is purely fact-oriented, so he doesn't normally express his feelings about faith or religious doctrines.

"Of course, he knows all the books and chapters of the Bible, plus quite a few scriptures and biblical characters and much of the history of various religions, particularly of the Mormon faith. More importantly," I added, "his life is an example of the Golden Rule in action."

"Kim," said Dustin, "can you tell me the books in the Old Testament?"

"Frontwards or backwards?" Kim asked.

"Let's just do them frontwards. Maybe I'll be able to follow you better."

So he did: "Genesis, Exodus, Leviticus . . ." It took about two minutes to name them all—adding all the New Testament books just for good measure.

"He hasn't logged into his mind all the scriptures verbatim," I explained, "but if you ask him about certain passages, he can usually locate them for you and try to explain the meaning of the scripture. He seems to be able to put the concept across in ordinary language and in a manner that is accepted."

Dustin addressed Kim again. "What's the tallest mountain in America, Kim?"

"Denali, Alaska—20,320 feet, thank you."

"Do you know the capital of Kenya?"

"Nairobi," came the answer, without the least hesitation,

punctuated by one of his earmark "Did you know that?"
quips.

Dustin then hummed seven or eight musical notes.

"You like Rachmaninoff?" Kim's eyes lit up.

Dustin let out a laugh. "Hey, Kim, give me a chance. I
wasn't to the recognizable part yet."

Then, as Kim rose from his seat and went back to his
pacing, Dustin asked, "What kind of schooling did he have?"

"He spent less than ten minutes in first grade. The teacher
and principal said he was too distracting, too hyper. He has
to pace quite a bit—he has lots of pent-up energy, and he
tends to talk out loud to himself.

"There wasn't an education act for children with
handicaps back in 1957. Today's law for people with learning
disabilities, P.L.94-142, didn't appear until 1975—too late
for Kim. We tried to get the school district to provide some
type of schooling for him, and finally they hired a couple of
retired teachers to come to our home twice a week for about
45 minutes per session. His first lesson was at age seven."

Dustin nodded to assure me that he was still listening. I
continued.

"Kim learned quickly. Before his official schooling began,
he had already learned how to add, subtract, divide, and
multiply, plus he could print and spell many words. In fact,
his vocabulary and grammar were excellent—skills he must
have developed through his reading and his contact with
adults. At 14, he had completed all the curriculum available
through high school, but he was never given a completion
certificate.

"Later, while I was working as public information officer
for the Utah State Office of Education, I asked the Utah State
Board of Education to consider him for a high school
diploma." (In early 1989, the Murray School District and the
Board of Education presented Kim with his graduation
certificate. The day before, the Utah State Legislature passed

a resolution commending him for his role in *Rain Man* and dedicated the day to Kim.)

"Fran," Dustin looked away in thought, "can you give me an idea just what Kim's problems are?"

"I can tell you as much as we know, including theories from several doctors who've spent time with Kim trying to figure him out," I replied.

I outlined in detail what specialists had unearthed from Kim's MRI brain scans and explained that Kim had also undergone several comprehensive ophthalmological assessments at that time. But the results of each of the exams was so different that the doctors concluded they couldn't determine what eyeglass prescription would help him improve his vision.

As I look back at those eye exams, I believe that when the examiners asked Kim to read the first line he could see clearly, he attempted literally to read it, trying to make sense of the jumbled letters as parts of actual words. But since it didn't make sense, he ignored it. In fact, for one line he tried to read

Kim and me with our new friends, Roger Bierbaum, Barry Morrow, Dustin, and Marty Brest, 1987

he told the optometrists that if they would change the next to last letter to a Z, they'd come up with the name of some obscure player I'd never heard of who played tackle on the 1937 Notre Dame football team.

"He's still wearing the same lenses he wore when he was 15 years old," I explained. "The frames have been changed three times. Sometimes he wears his glasses, sometimes he doesn't. He squints mostly out of habit. All in all, he seems to see quite well.

"When he's reading a paperback—one that doesn't contain a lot of facts or data he wants to remember—he turns two pages in about 12 to 15 seconds. Most readers read two pages in about two and a half to three minutes. Eye-reading tests reveal that he is able to read the left page with his left eye and the right page with his right eye, simultaneously, with over 98 percent comprehension. Most of us need some time to take in and consider what we are reading; with Kim, it's near instantaneous. He can also speed-read a single page using both eyes independently."

Dustin just sat there in lingering disbelief, wanting to hear more.

I went on to tell him that Kim spends more time on the pages of almanacs, maps and other things that require concentration for memorizing, probably using both eyes at the same time. He often makes grunts and droning noises, sounds that appear to be part of his concentration process, used to drown out outside distractions.

Then I explained Kim's difficulty remembering how to perform motor-skill tasks. For example, if he's shaving, after just a few strokes of the razor he'll forget how to do it. So I have to finish the job.

I've concluded that some of Kim's problems with these types of

KimKwip—We had paused to examine a large rose blooming in our patio garden: "Would we ever be able to make a rose? Especially a red one?"

everyday survival skills might be because he knows that if he wastes a lot of time on them, it will take away from the time he has to read and learn. Or maybe he's smarter than we give him credit for, in the motor skill-learning area.

"Some researchers are beginning to focus more studies on savants, but so far we've found only limited information," I offered.

Dustin interrupted my ramblings. "You mentioned 'autistic savants' earlier. Is Kim an autistic savant?"

I shrugged. "I don't think so. But I'm not that well informed on what autism is all about, just general information I've come across while studying retardation. Some of Kim's behavioral characteristics are certainly similar to autistic behaviors, but autistic individuals generally are antisocial loners, don't like to be touched or cuddled, and usually show little compassion towards others.

"As you can see, when he feels accepted, Kim is very social and loves people, especially children. The identified autistic savants who have been observed seem to demonstrate skill in one, sometimes up to three, general or technical-type subjects. One we know can calculate calendar dates, similar to Kim, but not as quickly; another can give you the square root of any number; another, blind savant can listen to a piece of music and then play it on the piano, note for note; and another can create perfectly proportioned clay sculptures of animals from memory."

"Can Kim do things like that?" asked Dustin.

"No, Kim's motor problems don't let him play a musical instrument, which takes a lot of coordination between mind and body. The absence of the corpus callosum may be one of the reasons he lacks the coordination, or the damaged cerebellum, but no one is able to say for sure."

I told them that instead, Kim can hear a musical selection from a record or tape, and even 30 years later hum it to you, describe it, and give you lots of facts about the composer. He

Kim, 1960

will also connect the piece to movie themes or other productions that have used the music.

Kim also enjoys reading record jackets, CD labels, and the information on cassette tape boxes. Plus he's read hundreds of books and catalogs on both classical and contemporary music. He remembers in what order the selections appear on the record or tape, the publisher, and, usually, the designs and colors of the label. He seems to have been unable to forget anything he's ever heard or read—ever since he was two to three years old.

"Unbelievable!" Dustin piped in. "How much does he read?"

"Much of the time. While he was growing up, he spent most of his waking hours reading. Every type of book:

histories, novels, almanacs, catalogs, telephone books, encyclopedias. And the information not only stays in his brain, but it seems to be filed away in 'association banks' for immediate recall.

"A word, a date, a person—any of them will trigger an association with some apparently unrelated topic. No one so far has been able to figure it out."

We have some 7,500 books in our home library and Kim's read most of them. How many other books he's read in other people's homes and in libraries, I couldn't estimate. He can recall nearly everything about a book, and he may also relate information from books to similar situations he's read about in newspapers or magazines, even if he read them many years ago.

Psychologists have asked me if Kim can tell the difference between fact and fiction, because he does read novels and some other types of fiction. Lots of times he can't. In his early years I'm certain he couldn't discriminate between the two. Everything was real to him, no matter how farfetched the story. But now, as he matures, it seems that he can better distinguish what's real and what's not.

As I finished telling all this to Dustin, Barry left the room and returned with two *Reader's Digest* condensed books, each with four or five abbreviated stories inside. Barry opened one to the contents page, looked Kim in the eye, and said, "Kim, I'm looking at *The Nun's Story*. What can you tell me about it?"

"It's the first book in the Volume 4, 1956 edition—written by Kathryn Hulme. Other books in that edition are *Merry Christmas, Mr. Baxter* by Edward Streeter; *The Success* by Helen Howe; *The Diamond Hitch* by Frank O'Rourke; and *The Sleeping Partner* by Winston Graham."

"Have you read any of those stories, Kim?" asked Dustin.

"Yes."

Dustin turned to Barry, a bit doubtful that he and Kim

hadn't rehearsed this little demonstration. "Barry, did you bring those books to the studio?"

Barry raised his arms above his head as if he was being robbed and lifted his eyebrows in an expression of innocence. "No! I noticed them in the reception room in the bookcase behind the secretary's desk when we came in. Kim did something similar in Texas when I first met him. Then when he came to my home, he told me about the stories in several of the editions I have."

Dustin paced back and forth. The room was totally quiet, until Kim again spurred on the discussion. "You'd like *The Diamond Hitch,* Dustin. It's about rodeos. *Midnight Cowboy! Midnight Cowboy!* You liked being in that movie?"

"I did. I really liked being in it," he replied, a grin bursting onto his face. Then Dustin hit me up for more details. "Tell me, Fran, what does Kim do all day long?"

I started at the beginning and gave Dustin an hour-by-hour account of Kim's activities. We get up pretty early, before 5:30. I have to help him use the electric razor, shower, and then we select the clothes he'll wear to work or to wherever we may be going that day. While dressing himself, more often

KimKwip—
Explaining one of his frustrations: "I couldn't sharpen my pencil. The hole in the sharpener was misplaced."

than not he'll put his shirt on backwards or his shoes on the wrong feet, so I do most of that work. Then I go downstairs, pack his lunch and fix breakfast. In a few minutes he comes down, minus his shoes, and sits down to read the morning paper—usually starting with the obituary section, looking for names and addresses he's memorized, and moving from there. All the while he asks dozens of questions about articles he's reading, even though I remind him over and over that I haven't looked through the paper yet.

When breakfast is ready, he immediately goes to the dining room table. He eats quickly and is usually stacking his dishes and carrying them to the kitchen sink by the time I sit down.

After breakfast and doing the dishes, we go back upstairs, where I put his shoes in the proper position and he puts them on. Then, together, we re-comb his hair and tuck in his shirt. Before we go out the door, he makes sure he has his lunch box and his notebook journal, which he'll take to the library after work. Around the time we met with Dustin, Kim was busy with a project entering data about people in both the United States and England, then matching up the surnames with people with similar names who lived in similar-size cities and who had the same last four telephone digits.

His main reference was a *Polk Directory*-like book, published in England in 1888, a book his grandfather gave him several years ago. Sometimes if population figures of two cities didn't fit together, he used the area sizes of comparably populated cities to connect them. Why he does this, I have no idea—but he seems to know. It's very complicated, and I haven't been able to discover many of the details of how he does it. Only Kim seems to understand the exact process, and he doesn't want to explain it.

KimKwip—Upon being handed the family cat, Quork, Kim addressed it firmly: "Don't throb on me. Kittens are supposed to be with their mother until they are older. Put him into his mother's hands."

"I'm out in left field when it comes to his journal projects," I admitted. "All I know is that they include a lot of names, numbers, and places, two areas in which his brain shows extreme interest." Then I added, "I believe his brain has to be working continuously, and this type of work keeps it at its peak."

(Since 1989, when Kim began his telephone book project, it has become evident that the matching of names and places has enabled him to study and memorize information listed in hundreds of directories from cities across America. His interest in memorizing metro telephone directories, however, has waned in the past few years, and he will no longer respond to questions concerning specific phone numbers or addresses. Still, he is able to describe roads and highways leading to and from almost every town or city, the area codes, ZIP codes, the town's main business firms and shopping outlets, historical events that have occurred in or near the city, and the television stations—by both channel number and call letters—that can be seen. If the city or town is west of the Mississippi River, he usually can tell you the three-digit prefixes of its telephone numbers. He also knows which telephone company serves each city.)

"And when does he read other kinds of books and magazines?" asked Dustin.

"Whenever he isn't at the library," I answered. "Sometimes when he reads at home he also watches television. But he always adjusts it to the lowest possible volume setting, or on mute, and watches in complete silence. At least I can't hear a thing. When I ask him how he knows what is being said, he tells me he can hear what's going on just fine. I assume he does. At least sometimes he'll laugh and giggle along with the people on the tube.

KimKwip—Offering me up a typical defense for why all his books were laying around his bed: "Do I have to put all my books back on the shelves? Some of them really need some fresh air."

"And, as you saw, he reads each month's volume of *Reader's Digest* condensed books and memorizes each week's *TV Guide*—wears the cover right off some of them; knows all the program schedules. In fact, he's mastered a certain way to hold the *Guide* and flip pages with his left hand while his right hand is busy twisting his cord.

"Often he hops from one book or magazine to the next, reading each for a few minutes before going on to the next one. He can read a page even if it's at an angle or upside down.

"When we visit someone in their home, the first thing he does is find the bookshelves and start leafing through their books. One thing that really gets him excited is coming across volumes he has in his own library.

"He twists his cord back and forth in front of his face and makes those droning noises while he reads. As I said, I think these are ways for him to relax as well as tools he's developed to deposit information into his brain."

Dustin kept up his pacing, looking first at the floor and then at the ceiling. Other than his feet scuttling along the carpet, the room was still.

"Do you pray, Kim?" Dustin finally asked.

"I bless the food at dinner sometimes."

"Do you ever pray to God to help you? Do you ever want to talk with God?"

Kim was quick to answer, though he didn't look up from the floor. "God is almighty. He knows my mind. Thank you."

Once more, silence.

"Excuse me, Kim," said Dustin, "I have to make another call."

As the busy actor went about his business, Kim rejoined the others, plopped down on a lounge chair next to the sofa, and asked Murray where he was from.

Murray hesitated. "You won't know where I was born because it's such a small place, actually a part of another city."

"What's the town?" Kim repeated more urgently.

"Concourse."

Kim's expression remained fixed, but his mind instantly snatched up the information. "You grew up in a small suburb of the Bronx. If you go north over the Brooklyn Bridge, then take Fifth Avenue onto Third Avenue and then go over the Harlem Bridge, you're home."

"Know the area code, Kim?" I asked.

"212, same as Manhattan. And you pay your phone bill to Ninex."

Murray was speechless.

"Where were your parents from, Murray?" I asked.

Murray hedged again. "He won't know where the town is because it changed hands after World War II."

"Let's give him a chance," I urged. "You might have to give him a clue or two if he asks for it. OK?"

Murray gave in. "Wilno," he said.

"Before the Yalta Conference in 1945," Kim started in without missing a beat, "Wilno was in Poland, just west of the border from Russia. After the conference, it was realigned inside the Russian border." Then Kim got a little more personal. "Murray, you must be a Russian Jew."

"You're right, I am," the writer marveled. "My folks migrated to the United States in 1946 and I was born six months after they settled in Concourse. I can't believe it."

"You can't believe what? What'd I miss?" asked Dustin after he had hung up the phone.

"Kim just told me about the place where my folks lived—first in Poland and then in Russia. It just isn't possible for anyone to know all the details of that time in history." His sudden respect for Kim's abilities brightened the whole room.

Spurred on by Murray's obvious fascination, Dustin scooted a chair up in front of the sofa, sat down, and leaned in. "Kim, my folks live in Los Angeles, in Rancho Santa Fe. Know where that is?"

"I do. My uncle lives in Carlsbad, near there."

Dustin leaned back, took a breath, and, his gaze still locked on Kim, spoke to Barry. "You know, Barry, when I first read your script, I figured it was a stroke of creative genius. No way was there a person who could do what you described."

"I had to invent several of the events, but Kim is presented just as he is," Barry

KimKwip—When asked about his taking the bus home from work: "Sometimes the bus driver doesn't recognize me when I'm not here."

On yet another occasion he failed to remember that, since he owns a bus pass, he doesn't have to pay to ride: "Dad, you owe the bus driver a quarter. He forgot I got off without paying the box."

explained. "When I met him a few years ago, I couldn't believe it either. Since then, he's learned a lot more things. At least it seems that way."

After a time, Dustin stood and stretched his legs. He spoke reluctantly. "Well, in about an hour and a half I have to be on a plane heading back to New York. This has been an experience no one will ever believe but me."

"And us," Murray corrected.

"Do you think you can direct a movie like this one, Marty?" asked Dustin.

"Can't wait to get started," Marty nodded.

Dustin then turned back and stepped towards Kim, and, extending his arms, drew him up off his chair. Still clutching Kim's hands, he said, "Kim, when you met me this morning you said that 'from this moment on we shall be as one.' I would like to say something to you, too. I may be the star, but you are the heavens."

In silence, Dustin and Kim touched noses as they embraced. Dustin's moist eyes remained focused on Kim's face for several seconds. Then he wiped his face with the back of his hand and turned and shook hands with Barry and me. He took my hand in both of his. "Fran, thanks so much for bringing Kim here so we could meet him. I might need some help from you in the next few weeks. I'd also like to see copies of Kim's journals, if that's possible. My office will be in touch with you soon. Again, thanks for your time and for one of the most incredible experiences I've ever had."

He made his way one last time over to Kim, threw his arms open, and pulled him close. "See ya, Rain Man!"

"Dustin, be the good man that you are!" Kim answered back as would a mother to her son, placing his hand on the movie star's arm.

Then, slipping his briefcase under his arm and with a cordial wave of the hand, Dustin disappeared out the door.

As far as extended personal contact was concerned, Dustin

had vanished. Yet, for Kim, he would forever be a close friend. And the memories of that special day with Dustin will always linger. For Kim and me it was an exceptional treat to meet such a remarkably sensitive person.

"Dustin is a great man," sighed Kim as we made ready to leave. "He will be remembered for many movies and stage appearances, but mostly, he will be thought of for being Rain Man."

Epilogue on a Day with Dustin

SINCE THAT EXTRAORDINARY DAY SPENT WITH DUSTIN AND his movie friends—now our friends, too—the pathway toward the making of *Rain Man* turned rocky. Marty Brest left the scene, whereupon UA/MGM attempted to hire Steven Spielberg, Sydney Pollack, and finally Barry Levinson to direct the picture. Dustin's dogged determination is ultimately what made the film a reality.

Then there were script rewrites. At least five times, the sequences from Barry's Morrow's original story were revised;

some were eliminated altogether, while new ones were added. But persistence eventually won out. Barry and Ron Bass combined their writing skills to finalize the script and, driven by the creative talents of Dustin, Tom Cruise, and Barry Levinson, the moving portrayal everyone was seeking came together.

Dustin is a very thorough technician. In every way possible he makes sure his roles are carefully prepared and thought out. Kim's authentic persona turned out to be too complex for the story to depict. So, prior to the production of the movie, Dustin sought out several autistic savants and observed their behavior tendencies. By mimicking their antisocial ways and blending them with Kim's more communicative nature, he gradually came up with the composite character of Raymond Babbitt.

> *KimKwip—Upon finding an edition he thought was lost: "The lump last night in my bed grew to be a TV Guide."*

During the film's production, Dustin sent Kim a black leather "Rain Man" jacket, which Barry Morrow presented to Kim at the New Mexico State Arc Convention in Albuquerque. He also sent us several autographed posters and a director's chair signed by himself, Tom Cruise, and members of the production crew. For his contributions to the film, Kim was also presented a trust fund established by Dustin. (However, because Medicaid is required as his sole source of hospital insurance and limits his assets to just over $2,000, his trust fund was taken from him by the courts, reduced by legal fees, then turned over to Kim's brother and sister.)

Months passed, and the time for *Rain Man's* debut finally arrived. Dustin invited us to Hollywood to attend the movie's premier and the reception that followed. The limousine ride from Barry's home, along with his wife and children, still brings back wonderful memories.

Later that year, Barry Morrow extended an invitation for Kim and me to come to Los Angeles for several pre-Academy Award festivities. After being honored at a lavish party hosted by Barry's sister, we all sat down to watch the show. Besides making many new friends, several reporters interviewed and filmed Kim during the evening.

As Dustin accepted his Oscar for Best Actor, the first thing he said was: "My special thanks to Kim Peek for his help in making *Rain Man* a reality." What a thrill for Kim!

As the awards kept piling up (Best Picture, Best Director, and Best Screenplay), Kim became so animated that several times he jumped right out of the range of the TV viewfinders as cameramen tried to capture his reactions for live broadcast. For an individual who in all his years in recreational classes at a sheltered workshop had never leapt more than a few inches off the ground, Kim's nearly three-foot hurdles across the floor gave me much pride. It was one memorable night!

Perhaps the most telling clue that Kim had overcome much of the isolation and fear that had plagued him most of his life was his response to the press that night. Columnists and camera directors were attracted to this young man's originality, his honesty, his complete lack of guile, his warm and lovable personality.

On the heels of *Rain Man's* Academy Award success, an interview was published in the *L.A. Times* by reporter Larry Christon. Christon had earlier sat next to Kim at the movie's premier and had also visited our Salt Lake home to complete his story. His outstanding, in-depth article captured a great deal of the uniqueness that is Kim. (Similar articles have since appeared in local newspapers across the country, describing not only Kim's singular savant capabilities but also addressing his newly developing confidence when out among people. A number of these articles are highlighted in the Appendix at the end of this book.)

KimKwip—
While gazing outside our patio window:
"Hearing a whisper is like wanting to kiss a hummingbird."

An award-winning TV biography, "Kim," was subsequently written and produced by Shelley Thomas, co-

Shelley Thomas and Kim, 1988

anchor of KSL-TV, the then CBS affiliate in Salt Lake City. It was televised on January 31, 1989, just as the movie was beginning to draw thousands of viewers to theaters across the country. It related beautifully the story of Kim's coming out. Shelly became another major influence on Kim's rather ceremonious entrance into everyday "social circles," and the relationship she shares with Kim became—and remains—a close one. Today, her documentary is regularly used as part of Kim's introduction at conferences and seminars. Or, often, when Kim is asked to interact at special events, Shelley will introduce him to the audience herself.

She is sometimes followed by Dr. Dan Christensen, director of the University of Utah Psychiatric Department— formerly the Western Institute of Neuropsychiatry. He was the person who first studied Kim's unusual mental state. In his introductions, he will explain about savants and describe the medical characteristics of Kim's brain and theories relating to his behaviors.

While coordinating other similar studies at research institutes across the United States, Dr. Christensen and his team continue to examine Kim's phenomenal abilities in the areas of memory and neuro-functioning. Dr. Christensen is another special friend who has had an important influence on who Kim is today.

KimKwip—An audience member will inevitably ask Kim his favorite line from the movie Rain Man. *He knows it will draw a loud response from the room, so he shouts, "I buy my underwear at K-Mart! Where else?"*

Into the Sunshine

FOLLOWING THE PUBLICITY GENERATED BY *RAIN MAN,* AT Dustin Hoffman's urgings and with Barry Morrow's comment that "the whole world needs to meet and know Kim" still ringing in my ears, I spent many hours soul-searching, weighing the prospects, good and bad, of turning Kim into a public figure. I thought of how Kim might react going out into the "sunshine" after living in the shadow of family and friends for so long. I thought of what we would be

Me, Kim and Barry in front of the Rain Man billboard,
corner of Hollywood and Vine, Los Angeles, 1989

Kim accepts "Mini-Oscar" from Dr. Dan Christensen, 1989

giving up—weighed against what we would be giving. Would the added notoriety hinder his studies or infringe on our privacy? And, in particular, I sought to gain a sense of the potential dangers of exposing Kim to large groups.

Although all the members of the family did not completely agree on my taking Kim from his closeted, protected world out into the light—and danger—of the big, real world, I decided the opportunities vastly outweighed the risks. At least I had to give him a chance. Both he and I had to see if he could build a new life in an environment filled with all kinds of people and unknown challenges.

Sure, I was concerned about the things he might say in public. And I was worried about what might be said about him—and to him—by those insensitive few. After all, Kim

had been labeled "retarded" (a label which had clouded his abilities and robbed him of his potential for 37 years). But I decided that Kim was strong now. And if something was said that I felt was offensive, I would just consider the source, not be angered, and, if appropriate, attempt to educate the person.

It was also of the highest priority for me that Kim not be seen as being exploited. So I decided not to ask for any fees for Kim's appearances, hoping that would eliminate that thought in anybody's mind. And more and more the impression came to me that sharing Kim with the rest of the world would do both the world and him a lot of good. I would be alongside him at all times as a "safety net," not just to protect him from comments or any sort of confrontation, but also to serve as moderator, interpreting his responses and helping him interact with his audiences.

So, my son and I went on the road. And if I had any fears or lingering doubts, those were quickly put to rest. As I had hoped, Kim remained "just Kim"—an unaffected, trusting, happy, articulate and brilliant ambassador for people with special abilities.

PART III

—————

Everyday Kim—
His Open-book Journey Continues

*American Bread, the French Connection . . .
and More*

KIM LOVES HIS NEW AND BUSY LIFE; HE DOESN'T SEEM AT all phased by the hustle and bustle. I often remind him that when he tires of the traveling, we'll quit. But so far he's thrived on being out among people. And the feeling is more than mutual. His audiences have been overwhelmingly cordial.

He becomes most animated when we visit schools and he's given a minute or two to "preach" to his young audiences on the basics of respect: "Moms, dads, teachers, old people, especially old people, they all have something called wisdom. It's something you'll get when you get older. But until you get it, you need to respect those who have it . . . "

Students are a bit tentative at first. Then, after sizing Kim up, they begin to gravitate toward him, drawn in by his uncanny data bank of knowledge. He answers each question in turn. If asked, he'll rattle off the states and their capitals in the order (or in reverse order) they were admitted to the Union, weaving in with each grouping of states the U.S. presidents who served at the time and the dates they held office.

Then, as the presentation progresses, the young people grow increasingly spellbound, won over by Kim's pleasant,

Kim with the children, 1991

wholesome, and innocent demeanor and his playful rejoinders:

> The auditorium was packed with hundreds of enthusiastic middle school students. Many had spent time in their libraries researching questions—most dealing with history—to ask Kim.
>
> He had already successfully answered over 60 of them, when a young girl came to the microphone, her question carefully printed on a small scrap of paper: "Kim, what can you tell me about Napoleon?"
>
> Kim glanced over at me, made a couple of grunting noises, and answered in his usual improvisational style, "Do you know what you get if someone throws a bomb into your kitchen? You get your 'linoleum blown apart'!" Then he broke out into a mini fit of throaty chuckles.
>
> A ripple of laughter swept through the auditorium; soon, even those who hadn't yet understood the pun joined in. Then Kim turned to me and said, "Dad, I wanted to give them a funny."

Corny, yes. But funny?
Absolutely!

When Kim goes off on a tangent (which is fairly often), I try to redirect him back to the original topic. Then I try to decipher for his audience what bit of information might have ambushed his mind and the sequential leaps of logic it might have taken from there:

A student once asked Kim who sewed the first American flag, and he replied that it was Betsy Ross in 1777 and that her design was formally adopted on July 14 of that year.
Then he added, a twinkle in his eye and a grin flashing across his face, "She could have finished it sooner if she hadn't had a second job baking all that bread." (Betsy Ross Bread, I explained to the befuddled audience—as Kim let loose an open display of glee—was a popular brand sold in Utah during the sixties.)

Kim is, in a way, a sort of role model. But he doesn't take himself too seriously. In fact, even though for him most things have to be either "yes" or "no," black or white, occasionally he displays a definite talent for comedy. He's learned to enjoy it when people laugh at something he might say. And once he succeeds in eliciting laughter as a response, the scene becomes a memory for him to recall with pleasure time and time again:

Kim's presentation delivered to about 80 fourth graders had gone well. One of the teachers had forewarned us that she had two boys in her class who were troublemakers and that they might mimic Kim's finger-in-front-of-his-face actions or some other behavioral trait he's not able to control.
Sure enough, at about the halfway point, one of these boys raised his hand and asked Kim how many stars there

were in the universe. Kim replied that no one really knows because, according to his readings at least, even our biggest telescopes can only see out to a point where there is literally a "wall of light." This wall is comprised of trillions of additional stars over and above those which astronomers have already mapped out.

The boy was impressed, but then asked if Kim knew how many missions the shuttle *Discovery* had made. Kim responded with 21, an answer which impressed the boy even more.

Afterwards, the teacher stopped me in the hall to let me know of this boy's positive reaction. He had clearly been mellowed by Kim's message and had told her that he thought Kim deserved more respect than anyone he had ever known.

Later, when I shared with Kim how he had helped this boy begin to appreciate differences in others, he moved close to me and placed his head on my shoulder. It was a touching gesture. And so I said to him, resting my head on his, "I love you, man." Immediately he backed away from me and, echoing the much-repeated line from the recent TV commercial, transformed the mood of the moment: "No, Dad, you can't have my Bud Lite!"

That's Kim!

And, last but not least, on one occasion he *took* the occasion to slam one of America's most bitter foes, giving him, if you will, a one-two *pun*ch:

We were busy interacting with a student assembly of about 600 lively middle school kids. Prior to Kim's visiting a school, students are asked to go to their library, find some good questions, and record the correct answers so they can check Kim's responses. They are also asked to identify the source of their information. (Besides being a fantastic learning opportunity for the students and a way to familiarize them with their libraries' resources, the combined mental calisthenics of thousands of students a month helps Kim absorb new details and keeps him on his toes!)

Well, this particular visit fell on the week after the United States and its allies had declared war on Iraq. Many of the school's students were wearing gold ribbons over their hearts in honor of those serving in Desert Storm.

The young student body officer assigned to introduce Kim opened up the questioning: "What do you think about the situation in the Persian Gulf?"

Kim's face took on a feigned meditative expression. Then, to scattered laughter, he answered, "Saddam's shame!"

Goin' for the Gold!

ARCHBISHOP TERENCE CARDINAL Cooke, while terminally ill with leukemia, reflected that "the 'gift of life,' God's special gift, is no less beautiful when it is accompanied by illness or weakness, hunger or poverty, mental or physical handicaps, loneliness or old age. Indeed, at these times, human life gains extra splendor as it requires our special care, concern and reverence."

I love this quote for what it says about Kim. It is a message he takes to the world

KimKwip—(March, 1996) As another school assembly wound down, I asked Kim if he had anything else he'd like to tell the students. After briefly restating his message, he surprised me with another, very thought-provoking plea that really touched these 13- and 14-year-olds: "I especially want you to love your little brothers and sisters, because they're going to have to do the same thing for their world as you're doing for your world—making it a better place to live."

now, but it is one he lived before *Rain Man*. Though Kim has, as it were, taken flight, he actually runs and walks using a somewhat penguin-like, slightly sideways motion. But he runs just the same:

It was a chilly morning in May of 1970 as Kim and I sat in the shadowed bleachers of the University of Utah football stadium. The inaugural Utah Special Olympics had invited Kim to participate in a 50-yard dash. A spirited 19-year-old, who just five years previous had learned to walk up and down stairs without assistance—and now here he was about to run a race.

Prancing in his sideways, crab-style shuffle onto the track, he was pitted against two young cerebral palsy victims confined to wheelchairs. Like Kim, each of these young men was anxious to take the gold medal.

The three of them were led to the starting line and the starter's pistol was raised skyward. As the shot rang out, Kim paused a few seconds as his two wheelchair rivals pulled away; then he began to bolt down the track. Soon he approached the finish line, well ahead of the other two struggling racers—one turning in circles in his effort to propel his chair, the other maneuvering down the track backwards, moving just a few feet at a time with an occasional push of his feet.

But then, no more than two yards away from breaking the ribbon, Kim stopped and turned around. His fellow runners were jammed together off to the side of the track, barely 30 yards down the course. Immediately he scurried back to them and pulled the wheelchairs apart. Then, very slowly, he pushed the first man through the ribbon. Next he returned to the other racer, straightened out his chair, and wheeled him across the line—in a photo finish of a different sort. Kim was a proud third-place winner of the 50-yard dash!

As he stood on the platform to receive his award, Kim tilted his head back and forth as Coach Jack ("Cactus Jack") Curtis of the University of Utah football team draped the bronze medal around his neck. Kim beamed with pride.

But the coach wasn't through yet. "Kim," he said into the microphone, "we hereby award you the most important recognition of the Special Olympics, the Sportsman Award for your unselfishness in helping your two friends win the gold and silver medals."

"Yes, and thank you," Kim replied, still smiling. Then,

eyeing the ground, he addressed Coach Curtis; he had something important to say: "You know, Coach Jack Curtis, you are a great man. But Utah has had better coaches."

Curtis' smile broadened and, with tears coursing down his cheeks, he reached out and drew Kim close.

I *Travel Incognito*

IN THE MID-'70S I VOLUNTEERED TO DEVELOP A KIT FOR the Governor's Council on Developmental Disabilities that would enable parents to teach their youngsters with disabilities about human sexuality—one-on-one and in the privacy of their own homes.

During this time, Kim and I were at a conference in Denver, learning about the problems facing parents whose children with handicaps were unfamiliar with many of society's norms. And one of the top priorities for these students' social education was human sexuality.

During the lunch break, Kim and I took a stroll down 16th Street—as we later discovered, one of the more chancy places to wander:

> The sidewalk turned out to be the gathering place for hundreds of transients and homeless men and women. With Kim holding my arm and his eyes fixed on the clouds and the tops of the buildings, apparently detached from the clamor and clutter around him, he shuffled alongside me down the street.
>
> Out of nowhere, an inebriated, disheveled man approached us, put his hand on Kim's chest, and looked directly into his eyes. In a quiet yet commanding voice the man sermonized, "My son, Jesus walks with you."
>
> Kim hardly broke stride, but lowered his eyes to meet the man's gaze. He would clear up this poor fellow's obvious misconception. "No," he shot back, "this is my father."

Innocence: The World Needs More of It

INNOCENCE? WELL, KIM IS UTTERLY CHILDLIKE WHEN IT comes to "adult" material:

> Attempting on another occasion to teach Kim about human sexuality using the table-top card kit, I came to the section dealing with the differences between young girls and mature women. Holding up a drawing of a young ten-year-old wiping her leg dry with a towel, followed by one of a mature woman with her more rounded curves and enlarged chest as she pulled her towel across her back and shoulders, I asked, "How can you tell the young girl from the older woman?"
>
> Kim looked closely at the illustrations, his eyes shifting back and forth. Then he announced, "Young girls always wipe their legs first and older women wipe their backs first."
>
> After no less than four subsequent attempts to teach Kim the fundamentals of human sexuality, I've finally decided to wait until he begins to inquire on his own about that sort of thing. Because he is such a compassionate man, always putting his arms around the ladies he meets and holding the hands of the men, I've managed over the years to teach him the basic do's and don'ts of social behavior. But a romantic he'll never be. As for what body parts are all about, his toothbrush is still one of his biggest challenges.

> *KimKwip—At the railroad crossing, a passing train held up our car for nearly 20 minutes: "Dad, how do railroad cars have babies?"*

(After my most recent attempt I asked Kim why he didn't want to learn about human sexuality via the kit. He remarked, "I don't want to grow up before I'm old enough.")

A Historical Bent

TODAY, KIM CONTINUES TO READ AND READ, FEEDING HIS memory's storehouse. Hordes of books, several of them open, lay about his bed nearly every evening. Finally about midnight, he restores them to their designated spots on the shelves and goes to sleep. Then about 5:15 A.M., he arises "ready for another beautiful day, Dad!"

He keeps himself updated on current events, often comparing and associating the day's happenings with similar events of historical significance. But too often the words— and their literal meanings—just get in the way:

> The exchange between Kim and a professor of American History at Utah State University had kept pretty much on course. For over an hour they had been discussing the plight of blacks from pre-Revolutionary times through the Civil Rights era, sharing information that was the result of thousands of hours of study.
>
> The entire Civil War period, with its many generals and battles, had dominated their conversation for just a few minutes. However, within those few minutes there surfaced one of Kim's most celebrated quips.
>
> "Well, Kim," said the amazed professor when the dialogue lagged a bit, "what do you know about Abraham Lincoln?"
>
> Kim began with Lincoln's date of birth, his death date, when and how he died, who he had married, his service in Congress, and so forth.
>
> "Very good," interjected the professor. "Can you tell me his Gettysburg Address?"
>
> "Will's House, 227 North West Front Street," Kim's voice rose again, almost without pause, "But he only stayed there one night. He gave his speech the next day."
>
> The professor chuckled at the dual meaning of the word *address* upon which Kim had pounced. He had been warned that Kim takes everything at face value, and now, firsthand, he had been an eyewitness of the fact.

Business groups, church gatherings, and youth organizations often invite Kim to speak at their meetings. Whenever possible, we oblige. Without exception, every visit has been positive and very appreciated.

Historical references play a big part in his presentations:

> The audience was made up of professionals and staff members from several intracity medical centers in St. Louis, Missouri. Kim had responded to questions touching on a number of subjects, when a man in a white lab uniform raised his hand. I recognized him and he asked, "What can you tell us about General Douglas MacArthur?"
>
> I expected Kim to mention the famed general's "I shall return!" passage, pronounced upon leaving the Philippines during World War II, or his parting words, "Old soldiers never die—they just fade away," when he retired from the military.
>
> But Kim's thoughts seldom imitate mine. I suppose because we were in President Harry Truman's home state, Kim felt a reference should include him. So he blended MacArthur's tone and one of the president's best-known sayings into a fictional conversation, ending with, " . . . MacArthur telephoned President Truman and said, 'Buck up, Harry. It doesn't stop here!'"

Grief Runs Deep When Children Are Abused

AN OLD GROUCH, ABOUT TO ENTER A BUILDING, FOUND that the heavy glass door was being held open for him by a little boy. "Never mind that," said the grouch, "I don't need your help." The child smiled up at him and said, "You're welcome."

Trauma or violence inflicted on children disturbs Kim immensely. An airplane crash that kills 300 adults sends him into near hysterics. However, if the newsman mentions that one baby was injured or killed, he goes into a tearful, almost uncontrollable tantrum. Struggling by every means to console him and help him contain his heartache—often by reminding him to count or breathe deeply—it may take 20 or 30 minutes to calm him down to where he can function.

When the emotional floodgates finally draw shut and we are able to put the hurt aside, he embraces me and tells me how much he loves me. I assure him that I, too, love him with all my heart:

> It began with a headline in the morning paper: MISSING CHILD'S BODY LOCATED IN CANAL. All at once Kim came stomping into the kitchen as if he were on a pogo stick.
>
> "What's the matter?" I asked. "Why are you upset?"
>
> Kim's face gave off an expression of anguish and he shouted uncontrollably: "Why was the baby wrapped up in its blanket and tied up with rope? So it wouldn't get wet? Why would the father bathe the baby with all its clothes on? Does all life begin in the water? I can't be wrapped in a blanket and thrown in a river. I'd catch cold!"
>
> Placing my arm on his shoulder, I guided him into the living room and sat down beside him on the sofa. But once more he leaped up, writhing in confusion, rubbing his hair and then gripping his hands tightly, twisting them until they seemed they would separate from his arms.
>
> I pulled him back onto the sofa and tried to comfort him. "It was a kookie thing, Kim," I said softly. "Whoever did it is sick in the head. Some people aren't able to cope with their problems and sometimes they do things that are bad. Sometimes they don't even know what they're doing."
>
> "Why, Dad? Why? That was just a tiny baby. He couldn't fight his father. You wouldn't hurt me like that, would you?"
>
> "Of course not, punk," I said, giving him a reassuring pat. "And maybe that dad didn't mean to hurt his baby, either. But he must have lost his cool and hit him without realizing what he was doing."
>
> My tender son was still unable to see the logic in it all—and, frankly, neither was I—and he looked to me for further

comfort. "But he wrapped him in a blanket and tied him up so he couldn't get loose . . . and then he put him in a canal. Why, Dad? How can a father do something like that?"

All in all, it was a rough morning. Kim was unable to keep his breakfast down. His breathing came in ragged puffs. He'd be quiet for a few minutes, then bolt to his feet and hit me up with the same kind of anxiety-filled questions.

It took over an hour to quell his fears. Afterwards, we went outside on the patio and stared down at the last drifts of snow still clinging to the low-cut foliage and skirting the wet walkways. "Want to take a stroll and breathe in some of that good air before we go to work?" I finally asked.

He replied sadly, "A short walk might be good for us, Dad."

He didn't say much as we tread in unison down the path, just let out a series of tired sighs. Neither was he his usual talkative self in the car as we drove to the workshop. Then, as I opened the car door to help him out, everything spilled out at once. "There are fathers who love their children all of the time, aren't there, Dad? And you are one of those, aren't you, Dad?"

He put his soft, heavy hand in mine, threw his other arm around my neck, and pulled my forehead to his. "Yes, Kim. I love you very much. No way could I ever harm you. You wouldn't hurt me, either."

He kissed me on the nose—real hard. "I'm going to have a good day, Dad," he said, at last giving the flicker of a smile. "If I have to call you to come and get me early, it will be because my body is very tired."

We walked together toward the workshop door. I could tell by his body language and his breathing that he was too exhausted to work. Inside, I explained to Kim's supervisor the events of the morning. Then I took Kim's arm and we plodded back over the icy parking lot to the car and drove home.

His ordeal had left him all wrung out, even too weary to walk upstairs to his room. All he could do was collapse on the sofa. And, to the snoring sounds of a long-awaited peace, I removed his shoes and covered him with a blanket.

A Jigsaw of Buttons and Buttonholes

K IM IS MORE MOTOR-RETARDED THAN MENTALLY RETARDED. For him, taking care of his own personal needs is a complex task. When shaving himself, he might, for instance, only finish one side of his chin.

Dressing oneself is another skill that demands the thinking of a "whole" person. And, on any given day, this is where Kim's impairments are most likely to show up:

> One morning, hurrying to get ready to leave for work, Kim came into my room "ready to go." The problem was unmistakable: his shirt was two buttons off and his collar stuck up high on his left side.
>
> "Guess what got past us this morning?" I asked.
>
> "What?" he instantaneously replied, sensing by my question and the tone of my voice that something was wrong with his appearance.
>
> "You've got your shirt buttons uneven and that makes your shirt crooked."
>
> Now Kim doesn't readily admit to being wrong about anything. So when I stood him in front of the mirror and tried to explain the problem, he responded rather brusquely, "Today, Dad, I wanted to look more horizontal."
>
> We rebuttoned the buttons anyway.

The Wild Ride off the Deep End

K IM'S MIND GOES OFF ON PERIODIC FLIGHTS OF spontaneity—wonderfully delightful journeys. Then there are the other times, incidents that send his imagination hurling off the proverbial "deep end." And usually he takes me along for the ride:

> Kim was much intrigued—and perhaps a bit on edge—

when news articles began appearing describing the tactics of the "Unabomber," infamous for sending packaged, ready-to-detonate bombs through the mail. So it was with some apprehension Kim found a package by our back door one day. I followed him from the carport to the patio, picked up the package, read the label, and said, "It's a Federal Express delivery."

"Who's it from?" A sense of alarm had crept into his monotone delivery.

"It was shipped from Scranton," I replied, "but it doesn't have any description of what's inside."

This must have made him even more worried. "If it's from the Unabomber, Dad, you need to fill that garbage can with water and drop it into it while I phone 911!"

I tried to explain that it probably contained some photos and other items from a recent trip we had made to Pennsylvania, but Kim wouldn't be convinced. "Open the door, Dad; let me watch from inside as you open it out here."

Good news: Enclosed were a tour guide of Scranton and several photographs from one of the many new friends we had met there. Kim grinned broadly and said, nodding, "They're good people back there, Dad. But why would they try to scare me?"

At times "the ride" gets awfully bumpy. More than once Kim's outspokenness has caused me to cringe:

Kim had learned of the death of Joey, one of his co-workers at his sheltered workshop. On the day of the viewing, he surprised me by suggesting we go.

We arrived a little early and found ourselves standing alone with Joey's mother at the foot of the casket. The mother was quite moved that Kim had come to pay his respects. "Come look at Joey," she greeted, taking Kim's arm and gently ushering him toward the body of her son. "He looks so peaceful, doesn't he?"

Kim's blunt reply hung in the air for more than a few awkward moments: "Sound asleep, just like at work every day."

Beauty Is *In* the Beholder

CONFUCIUS, KNOWN FOR HIS WISE PROVERBS, TRULY outdid himself when he made the statement: "Everything has its beauty, but not everyone sees it." Kim does indeed see beauty in most everything and in just about everyone he meets:

Six or seven youngsters with multiple handicaps attended the special preschool center in Charlotte, North Carolina, where Kim and I visited with 95 guests of the Charlotte chapter of The Arc (Association for Retarded Citizens). The severity of the handicaps these children suffered were enormous. But to Kim the impairments were of little importance. These were just sweet little kids and, longing for them to feel the compassion that flows from his heart, he sat down on the floor and began playing with them.

Something happened then that burst Kim's serene bubble. When the TV cameraman asked him to pick up a beautiful, long-haired four-year-old girl who had been severely brain-injured in an accident, Kim resisted. A staff member gently lifted the young girl and placed her into Kim's arms while the cameraman set up his position. Still too overwhelmed or frightened, Kim simply couldn't bring himself to hold the tiny child, almost dropping her to the floor.

Then, displaying a sense of urgency, Kim got up and made his way over to a young boy, his body dwarfed and his face shriveled. About four years of age, he bore a strong resemblance to the hunchback of Notre Dame. Kim promptly reached down under the boy's arms, picked him up off the ground, and drew him up to his chest. Turning toward the TV camera, he said, "The hearts of many people have not met this young fellow. He needs to be known. He needs to know love from many."

Looking directly into the youngster's somewhat panicked eyes, Kim then added, "You are just a little man on your way up. Grow in strength. Be your best." This said, he squeezed the boy tightly—apparently tight enough to force a loud and lengthy explosion from the child's bottom. Kim's eyes widened and he stared down into the face of the little boy, chuckled, and said, "I didn't mean to unlock all your potential!"

A few wet eyes joined the laughter. The TV people then walked over and helped situate the boy back onto the floor, after which the lady reporter gave Kim a hug and a kiss on the cheek. "Thanks, Kim," she said, peering into his eyes, "and please come back again."

His Ears Cast an Amazingly Wide Net

IF YOU WANT TO SEE SOMETHING YOU'LL NEVER FORGET, JUST come and observe Kim as he watches television. There he sits, the audio turned to mute, with telephone directories and reference books positioned all around him on the bed. While faithfully continuing to gather and record his phone facts, every minute or so he switches channels with his remote, still fully aware of everything else going on around him.

He'll intermittently break the rhythm of his work to talk to me, all without missing an address or phone number he's holding in his mind or something being "said" on the TV set. In other words, he possesses an extremely acute sense of hearing, due perhaps to damaged eardrums that function at a higher frequency than most people's.

A prime example of how Kim uses this gift is when we're eating in a restaurant. As we chat back and forth, it's not at all out of the ordinary for him to take off on a totally separate topic. When I ask him what he's talking about, he'll waggle a crooked finger toward a table two or three booths away and say, "Those two guys know what I'm talking about." Then, his super-sensitive ears evidently still fixed on his fellow diners' ongoing discussions, he'll renew our conversation—or pick back up on the next table's conversation—at will.

To me, this is one of the most amazing of his mind's abilities: its "multiple receptor capacity"—to be able to simultaneously function at the needed level and concentrate on as many items as he chooses:

> On one occasion I exited Kim 's room as he was busy studying his phone directories and reading another reference book, all while watching TV. A few seconds later, however, he came scampering into my bedroom, screaming excitedly, "Dad, did you see that hole-in-one? (I hadn't.) It was Trevino! The flag jumped right up and caught the ball!"

Tchaikovsky Would Have *Loved* It!

KIM'S GOT A WAY WITH PEOPLE—BUT SOMETIMES HIS "WAY" is way out:

> It was nearly time for the start of Kim's visit with a gathering of churchgoers in a small town west of Salt Lake. With approximately 60 persons in attendance on this hot summer evening, the sun was still fairly high in the sky and the chapel's double doors had been propped open to allow some circulation.
>
> Just then, in the doorway—and blotting out most of the opening—stood a short but very stout woman. Kim immediately spotted her and began to hurry down the aisle in her direction. Not knowing what his intentions were, I sped up to him and took his arm, drawing him to a stop.
>
> "I want to go talk with that lady in the doorway," Kim persisted.
>
> "We won't have time," I replied. "The meeting is about to begin."
>
> But just then a couple situated near the middle of the chapel captured my attention with a question, whereupon Kim again ambled off and in no time was standing alongside the woman, who by now was flushed with

laughter amid musical strains coming from Kim.

Approaching them and waiting until Kim had finished his song, I asked the woman what Kim had said to her. "I'm not sure," she answered with a smile, "but he did ask me how many children I had and I told him I had fourteen. Then he laughed and started in on that song he's singing now. I'm not sure what it is, although it does sound familiar."

The tune was from Tchaikovsky's *Nutcracker,* "The Buffoon Lady," played in the scene where the lady is in her full skirt and her youngsters are cavorting and dancing beneath it. Actually I was thankful this woman—whose hearty laugh soon gave way to a high-pitched falsetto cackle which shook the floor for several yards all around—didn't understand what Kim was doing.

A little impatient to get started with the program, and anxious to get the woman out of earshot in case Kim said something out of line, I offered to escort the woman to a seat. Exhaling heavily and dabbing her eyes, she thanked me, and I took Kim's hand to lead him back down the aisle to the front of the chapel. But he insisted that he had to tell the woman one more thing. I cringed and hurriedly whispered that it had to be something nice. He assured me that it would be.

Making his way back over to her, he reached down into the pew and took both her hands to lift her up, in the process almost toppling forward onto her. Unable to raise her from the bench, he exclaimed, "You're too close to hug, my lady, but you have well-protected bones."

Again, great bursts of laughter rose from the woman's chest as I pried Kim away to get on with the presentation.

It's Not "Weather" But **How** You Say It

As I've mentioned, Kim worries about the weather— I mean really worries about it! Why, we don't know, but when the clouds darken and drop down to hug the valley floor, or when the weatherman predicts a blizzard, Kim becomes preoccupied with opening all the drapes and the doors—on both sides of our home—so he can keep tabs on the skies.

It is during these times that I'm glad I can be there with Kim. He needs support not only to pass through life's figurative tempests, but also when he's enduring the literal storms. It's gratifying to be able to offer my personal guarantee that, yes, the sun will come up again in the morning:

It had snowed much of the night; about six inches of light powder covered our patio. Kim had been up and down the stairs several times, checking on the status of the storm.

Then about 5:00 A.M., just before it was time to get up and get ready to go to work, he trudged into my bedroom, sat down on my arm, cupped his large hands around my face, peered into my eyes from about six inches away, and whispered, "Dad, being with you is so important to me. You are the father of my heart."

Kim, out and about, 1993

And Where Is Dreamland? (Weather Update II)

WIND, RAIN AND DARKNESS MAKE MORE VIVID OUR FEARS and our frettings more passionate:

> KimKwip—
> Spoken on a
> particularly
> blustery evening:
> "Listen, Dad . . .
> the wind is gruff
> tonight."

It had been a long night. Kim had been unusually restless on account of the heavy rains and claps of lightning. Each time the thunder would roll over our house, he would be in my room, sitting on my arm or leg and assuring me that it was just a routine storm and would be over soon.

Each time I agreed and escorted him back into his room to tuck him in. As soon as his breathing became heavy, I would return to my own room.

About 4:00 A.M., my bedroom light came on and in shuffled Kim. He sidled over to me and sat down on the bed, cupped his head in his hands, and said, "Dad, I was frightened. I woke up and was nowhere to be found!"

I moved to the other side of the bed to let him curl up next to me into his usual fetal position, and soon he had snored off into his dream-world.

For a long while I lay awake, wondering what things must race through the microcosm of his mind. I'll keep trying to understand—but I'll probably never really know.

Oh, Say, Mozart, Can You Sing?

KIM SEES THINGS 180 DEGREES DIFFERENTLY FROM MOST people, in my mind a weakness he's managed to turn into somewhat of a strength.

Words and their associated meanings don't follow the same track for Kim as they would most of us. And his resultant ability to turn a phrase completely around both astounds and amuses. It's another way in which, despite his mental limitations in some areas, he seems to make up for them in others:

We were gathered outside the main building of the Shakespearean theater in Cedar City, on the campus of the College of Southern Utah. It was the opening night of the new season and one of the great benefactors of Utah had presented the festival with a beautiful water fountain which had been precisely designed to blend in perfectly with the breathtaking desert surroundings.

Following the dedication of the magnificent fountain, the audience entered the theater and took their seats. Scott Matheson, the state's governor at the time, prefaced the upcoming performance by commenting on the graciousness of the fountain's donor, one of Utah's philanthropists Dr. Obert C. ("O.C.") Tanner. He continued: "We should be honoring O.C. Tanner tonight for his special gift to this festival... Dr. Tanner, would you come up and say a few words before the play begins?"

But in place of Dr. Tanner, his wife approached the microphone. "I have to apologize for O.C.," she explained. "He has laryngitis and can't speak above a whisper."

What happened next ... well, you would have had to have been there. Instantly a voice was heard coming from someone in the front row. It was Kim, calling out, "O.C., can't you say?!"

When the meaning behind Kim's remark had sunk in, most of the audience burst into laughter and applause. Then the governor strolled away from the mike and towards the sound of the voice, reaching out to Kim, who stood to greet him.

"You're a great man, Scott Matheson," Kim gestured, smiling and taking the governor's hand, "even if you don't build fountains."

Governor Matheson nodded in agreement and ambled back over to the mike. "Maybe we should all stand and sing the 'Star Spangled Banner'?"

And we did.

Audiences will frequently ask Kim what he can tell them about Mozart, and more often than not he'll holler out the customary answer: "You forgot to name the other four!" (again, an association that is at first lost to his listeners but is very familiar to him).

Since this response leaves his audience totally in the dark, I always have to explain. The story harkens back to the 1985 Academy Awards when Sir Laurence Olivier was selected to announce the nominees and winner of the Oscar for Best Picture. Olivier, clearly nervous as he rushed onstage, stepped up to the podium, took the mike, tore open the envelope and announced, "The winner is *Amadeus!*"

As Kim well remembers, the sterling actor "forgot to name the other four" nominees.

Mindful of Hummers and Whirlers

KIM HAS ALWAYS BEEN FASCINATED BY THE SPACE PROGRAM, is knowledgeable about the history of NASA, and keeps pace with the pending launches and scientific experiments carried on the shuttles.

Well, back in the mid-'80s, one of Kim's chores at his sheltered workshop in Salt Lake was to assemble packets of plumbing O-rings. And so it was that when the space shuttle *Challenger* exploded in a ball of flames 74 seconds after liftoff on January 28, 1986—and its O-rings were presumed to be the cause of the tragedy—one spring morning several months later Kim and I were out in the garden:

> I noticed a large hummingbird hovering outside the glass of our kitchen window, trying to make contact with some of the plants on the inside windowsill. I called for Kim to come see. Gazing in wonder at the nimble and colorful bird, Kim tilted his head to one side and said, "Dad, that's a real whirler. I hope its 'O-rings' are working properly!"

Some years later, after the Gulf War had ended, we picked up on another discussion centered around hummingbirds:

> Attracted to the sugar-water feeders on our patio and in the backyards of adjoining homes, quite a few hummingbirds roam the neighborhood. I pointed out to Kim a particularly large one sipping at one of the feeders. "That's a real hummer, Dad!" he piped up. "You know that General Schwarzkopf had a white one to ride in during the Gulf War?"

Wisdom Is in the Eye(teeth) of the Beholder

LINUS PAULING TAUGHT THAT "THE BEST WAY TO HAVE A good idea is to have a lot of ideas." Well, then Kim must come up with more than his share of good ideas every day, because he sure has a lot of them! And how he comes up with some of them is beyond me:

It was the summer of 1990, and Kim's teeth had just gotten their annual cleaning. The dentist took me aside into his office and closed the door. "His teeth seem fine, except he has two deep cavities in two of his wisdom teeth in the lower jaw," he explained. "I would recommend that we contact an oral surgeon and have him take a look at them."

We made an appointment for a later date.

When on the appointed day we walked into the dental office, Kim was still bombarding me with less painful alternatives to having his "mouth butchered by a dentist who had never even seen him before."

I patiently tried to put him at ease. "Today we'll just have your wisdom teeth examined."

He appeared stunned. "Does he have to take them out of my mouth to look at them?"

"No, he'll probably have to X-ray them, like Kenny [our family dentist] did. But this time, if he puts those little cardboard squares of X-ray film into your mouth, don't crunch them in half!"

Kim defended himself. "My tongue was guarding the back of my eyes, which caused my mouth to bend the X-ray films."

"OK," I nodded, "but this time, try real hard to just leave them where the dentist puts them."

After mangling nine X-ray films, the dentist decided to check Kim's teeth and jaw with an X-ray scanner and forego placing the film into his mouth. It worked. Kim didn't move a muscle for nearly six minutes while the scanner rotated around his head. The relieved dental assistant scheduled the surgery to remove all four teeth for the next Wednesday morning at eight o'clock.

For five long days I heard every excuse known to man for leaving his wisdom teeth as they were: "They don't hurt . . . They don't have to chew . . . They don't smile when I do . . ."

Wednesday came—at last!—and as we walked into the small waiting room at the clinic the dentist was there to greet us—much to Kim's distress.

"After a few breaths of a special gas," the dentist explained, "we can remove the teeth and you will be able to go home about two o'clock. Is that OK, Kim?"

"What kind of gas?" Kim grimaced. "Mustard? Will it eat my heart out? Is it the same kind they used on the Cambodians?"

The surgeon, smiling, laid his hand on his jittery patient's shoulder. "No, it's a type of anesthetic. We've used it hundreds of times. Not a single case of anything going wrong."

Despite the overwhelming odds, Kim was still ready to do just about anything to delay the procedure—so he began to reminisce. "When my dad got his wisdom teeth taken out, just before he was drafted into the army, he had to give his dentist a 'C' stamp to buy the gas."

"Rationing—gas rationing time. Early in World War II," I explained to the surgeon and his two aides.

The dentist again held up the mask and hose connected to the tank and tried to calm Kim's nerves. "No, Kim," I interrupted, "it isn't that kind of gas. This gas is like ether and you know all about ether. It's going to be just fine. In a short while we'll go home where you can rest and read."

About an hour and a half later, Kim appeared in a wheelchair with the dental surgeon and a couple of nurses alongside. "Let's go over to the recovery area for about an hour so we can make sure everything is all right," said the dentist.

Kim's mother and her husband joined us in the waiting

room. "Hi, Mom!" Kim brayed, now much more at ease. "Banged all four of them!"—and he pointed to his mouth.

"And everything went just perfectly," said the doctor, handing me a small bottle containing the teeth.

An hour later, his head still draped in ice bags, Kim said goodbye to his mom and we headed for home.

Every half hour we changed the ice bags; no pain killers were needed. When dinnertime came around, he was ready to eat some mashed potatoes and gravy and a bowl of vanilla pudding.

Next morning, after his eight-o'clock mouth flush (called for once an hour all night long), he ate a breakfast of soft-boiled eggs and bread, then spent the day sprawled on the couch reading a dozen or so books. Crouching down onto the floor beside him, I said, "I was very proud of how you handled this serious operation, Kim."

"Yes, Dad," Kim smiled. "In my heart you were there. I could feel your presence inside my mouth."

. . . Perched on top of a stereo cabinet in our living room is a small 3 x 5-inch gold frame. Inside, mounted on maroon velvet, are Kim's four plucked teeth, symbols of an important chapter in his life. I guess you could say the display represents his personal "red badge of courage."

Weathering the Storm (Update Number III)

I'VE OFTEN THOUGHT IT IRONIC THAT MY RAIN MAN IS frightened by rain. If the forecast calls for storms of any type, he'll insist on checking the sky every few minutes:

"Will it saturate our roof and leak into our house?" he asked for probably the umpteenth time during one impressive downpour.

"Of course not, Kim. We've discussed this dozens of

times. Somehow you have got to make yourself quit worrying about the weather. It's outside; we're inside. It can't come into our home."

He looked at me, visibly assured, then picked up his dinner napkin and replied happily, "You must be right, Dad, the napkin is still dry!"

> **KimKwip—**
> *Worriedly surveying a darkening sky: "It's not the weather that's bothering me, Dad. It's the blue sky which I can't find."*

To the Smithsonian, James!

I T WE DON'T CHANGE DIRECTION, WE WILL ARRIVE AT WHERE we are going." This rather profound observation by Richard L. Evans is at once a commendation and a chastisement. In a sense, it's a slap in the face directed at mankind's often haphazard, casual attitude toward life. At the same time its moral encompasses a slap-on-the-back tribute to mankind's need and ability to succeed. And it's a declaration that, for good or bad, also applies to Kim: usually he's not too worked up over one particular thing, but once he gets an idea into his head that he wants something, he's relentless.

So it was with Kim's desire to visit the Smithsonian Institute in Washington, D.C.:

> In 1973, Kim, his mother, and I visited Washington, D.C., as part of a hastily planned trip down the East Coast. On the spur of the moment, we decided to take a bus tour of the capital city, which was to include an all-too-brief hour-long visit at the Smithsonian.
>
> However, before arriving at the museum—arguably the most comprehensive and prestigious in the world—the bus's air conditioning system went out. The temperature inside soon hit close to one hundred and, unable to find a replacement bus, our driver drove us past the Smithsonian and directly back to the cool comforts of the hotel.
>
> Kim, naturally, was disappointed, and said to the driver

as he exited the bus, "Someday we will return to this Smithsonian Institute and I will discover many things people have misplaced for all people to find."

"Yes, Kim, someday we will come back," I promised.

In the fall of 1994, between presentations at the University of Maryland Psychology Department, Kim and I returned to the Aero Space and Historical buildings at the Smithsonian. But having already had our fill of buses, during this visit we were chauffeured in an air-conditioned Cadillac.

A Touch of Mussolini

KIM'S COME A LONG WAY. FOR SOMEONE WHO IS SUPPOSED to lack a sense of humor, he says some of the most hilarious things I have ever heard.

And as his socialization opportunities expand, a definite awareness of comedy-producing situations is becoming more a part of Kim's personality and speech. His mind is so quick that sometimes he'll blurt out some teasing quip or subtle insight that might even take me several hours to catch:

> "Maybe you will always be a fascination, Kim," I said to him one day. I could see his eyes sparkle as some kind of a pun began to form in his head. "You know, Dad, Mussolini was in charge of a fascist nation!"

Dramatic flashes of humor flare up all the time now. In fact, puns have become a regular feature of Kim's social repertoire:

> Kim had spent nearly an hour answering questions and discussing events in American and British history with some 200 local hospital employees. Then we took the opportunity to see some of the work the staff did.
>
> The blood bank was the first place we visited. A

supervisor there explained the function of the centrifuge in separating out the blood's components, described the different types of blood stored for emergencies and for patients requiring transfusions, and demonstrated how the specialized scanners and microscopes matched and determined the status of each vial of blood. Then he asked, "Do you have any questions?"

"No," Kim answered, "but I want to thank you for inviting Dad and me to your hospital and for showing us all about your blood things." Then he added, trying to disguise the hint of a wry smile, "You know, you are the first hemosexual I've ever met!"

Kim vs. Computer

KIM'S CALENDAR CALCULATIONS SPILL OUT OF HIS MOUTH in such a stuttering, rapid-fire delivery that it's sometimes hard to catch all of his answers. At some of his school assemblies, he will tell dozens of students the day of the week they were born, this year's day their birthday falls on, and the day of the week and year they will turn 65, all in about ten seconds each. Any date, any year, back into the past or forward into the future, the answer is on the tip of his tongue in a fraction of a second.

One newspaper columnist, after interviewing Kim, opened his article with the statement: "The information stored in Kim Peek's brain would put most personal computers to shame…" In one instance, it literally did:

Kim was scheduled to appear on a local radio talk show. The station's two resourceful DJs had set up a contest pitting his brain against a computer loaded with perpetual calendar software. The DJs were even taking gag bets as to which of them would come up with the answers first.

The conversation started out something like this:

DJ: "Kim, we're going to give you three dates: one from history, another from current times, and a third from the future. At the same time my partner will type the dates into the computer, and the race will begin, OK?"

Kim: "OK."

DJ: "On what days of the week did or will these three dates fall: January 14, 1830; July 22, 1994; and February 13, 2051?"

Kim: "A Thursday, a Friday, and a Monday." He answered with no hesitation whatsoever—actually answering each as the date was read. The DJ stammered slightly, then explained that they were still entering the dates into the computer.

A half-minute later the results came back: "Thursday . . . Friday . . . and Monday."

"You Had Better Listen to Him, Kitty!"

KIM'S NATURAL AFFINITY FOR ANIMALS COAXES SOME tender feelings and comments out of him that otherwise would be left unfelt and unsaid:

For several months our 16-year-old cat, Quork, much loved by Kim and myself, had been hobbling about on badly crippled hind legs. She wasn't in any pain, but knowing she wouldn't be long for this world, we regularly gave her an extra amount of attention.

One morning, I walked into the dining room as Quork darted (as spryly as she could) into the house when Kim opened the patio door. Kim, knowing the cat only comes into the house when it's cold outside, picked her up by the neck and, holding her only an inch or two from his face, delivered a friendly scolding. "When you grow up," he hissed in mock anger, "stay around the patio so your cat food won't dry out!"

When Quork died a few months later, Kim asked me what we were going to do with the several cans of cat food left in the cupboard. After some discussion, we decided to bury them next to Quork in our patio garden.

We still miss her cuddles.

> *KimKwip—We stopped at a diner near the highway to have a soda pop. Staring at a discarded tire resting a few feet off the road, Kim said, "That driver must be driving really funny!"*

The One That Got Away

KIM HAS SUFFERED VERY LITTLE ILLNESS, WHICH MIGHT BE attributed to his lack of exposure to people during his childhood. He contracted measles and chicken pox along with his brother and sister and the other kids on the block, but a serious disorder just never cropped up (knock on wood!).

But we've been lucky, because to try to find out if he hurts anywhere isn't much different from asking your pet dog the same question. He's not a complainer; what's more, he simply can't tell you. We've also been lucky because the doctors were unsure just how long Kim might live.

That luck reminds me of a spring day and Brian, Kim's

younger brother, who collected butterflies as a hobby. You could always see him running up and down the roads in the nearby canyons snaring with his net all types of winged creatures. His collection, mounted in frames, was a fine one:

> Our stroll through the botanical gardens at the university campus had been pleasant and uneventful. It was the spring just after Kim had reached his twentieth year— a happy time for all of us, especially since doctors had said his life expectancy might only take him into his teens.
>
> Well, this particular day, as we made our way back on campus, Kim, breathing heavily after running up and down the walk, plunked himself listlessly down on a bench. Soon he had directed his attention to the flipping motion of the fingers of his left hand and making short, motor-revving noises, apparently deep in thought.
>
> Suddenly, a large orange and black-spotted Monarch butterfly floated boldly past his hands. As his eyes captured the streak of color flashing near his face, a smile crept across his lips and he chortled, "It must be the one Brian missed!"

Kim on the lawn with a butterfly, 1957

"Goodnight, Dad . . ."
(Tempest in a Teapot, Final Update)

K IM CAN BE BOTH EXASPERATING AND ENTERTAINING—
often at the same time:

The foothills above and the valley below our home had endured windy and snowy weather most of the day. That evening Kim had a hard time getting to sleep. Just when at last it appeared that he had nodded off and I had left the room, he jerked awake, followed me into my room, pushed me back onto the bed, and hunkered down on my chest.

Surprised by this unusual display of vitality, I let out a groan, then reached up and tried to force his rump up off the ribs he was about to crack. "Are you OK, Kim?" I murmured when I had caught my breath. "I checked the

On vacation; the kids outside a cabin
at Yellowstone National Park, 1957

weather a few minutes ago, and it stopped snowing."

"My dreams were not about what I wanted them to be about," he whimpered, adding, "But everything is all right now, Dad, because in my heart I know you are here with me. I can feel your hair tickle my teeth."

> **KimKwip**—*An impressive gush of water flowed from one of our downspouts. Kim, looking on safely from the window, sought a solution to the heavy downpour: "You know, floods can be born from lake effects. We should try to keep them apart."*

Shaking my head in a blend of amusement, wonder, and weariness, I slid him over to the side of the bed, stood him up alongside me, placed my arm about his shoulder, and walked with him back to his room. He immediately rolled onto his bed, and I struggled a bit to pull the tangled covers from under him. After remaking the bed, I folded back the comforter and watched from out of the shadows as the moonlight coming through his partially opened window blinds sparkled in his big blue eyes. Then I bent down and kissed him on the forehead. "Sleep tight, buddy," I said under my breath. "And I'll go comb my hair so it won't tickle your teeth anymore."

"Goodnight, Dad," he mumbled in return. "I hope you don't have to wake me up again until morning."

Gramm-Rudman, Beware!

KIM REALLY CARES—FOR CHILDREN, FOR THE ELDERLY, for the needy . . . for people in general:

"Will it mean that all our meat supplies in America will be no good after Monday?" Kim's shouts filled the house. "Will we give up on all our troops in the Persian Gulf? What about the older people who have to have their Social Security checks to stay alive? Are we going to let them starve?"

The Gramm-Rudman Act was about to go into effect to cut federal programs. Meanwhile, the final day for Congress to take action on the budget deficit and allocate funds for 1990-91 was fast approaching. And Kim…well, he was deeply concerned, and almost ill at this, his latest apocalyptic vision of disaster casting its long, ominous shadow across the lives of innocent people.

For two nights in a row he had sat on the edge of my bed and, every hour or so, stewed over the future state of the homeless, the elderly, the lower-totem pole government workers. No matter what I said to assure him that things would work out, his mind would flash back to similar tragic situations which had occurred over the past two centuries.

On Sunday morning, the last day of the government's fiscal year, the word was broadcast that Congress had passed a temporary settlement on the national budget. On hearing the news, Kim's eyes brightened and the corners of his mouth turned up. His voice echoed with pleasure: "I knew it would happen like this!" Then he took my hand and said, "Dad, people who really care about people shouldn't frighten them with Gramm-Rudman scenarios. What can we do about leaders who don't get their responsibilities attended to when they should?"

I put my other hand over his and said, "Maybe they just need to talk with you."

"When?" he asked—as usual, taking my remark at its utmost word.

"It's Sinking! It's Sinking!"

ONE SCENE IN *RAIN MAN* SHOWS CHARLIE TRYING TO convince Raymond to fly with him to L.A. As the kidnapped Ray repeatedly balks at the idea of boarding a plane—all the while citing dates and casualty numbers for various airline crashes—Charlie, exasperated, finally agrees to make the trip by car instead. Stalking back down the concourse, his brother dangling from his arm, Charlie goes berserk:

Charlie: "You're killing me, Ray! I just want you to know, you're killing me, man . . . "

Raymond: "No flying."

Charlie: "No flying."

Raymond: "'Course, I've got *Jeopardy* at five o'clock . . . "

Charlie: "Don't start with that, Ray . . . "

Raymond: "*Jeopardy* at five o'clock . . . "

Nowadays, Kim and I are on the road some 32 weeks out of the year, speaking to thousands of people. Our coast-to-coast travels, however, aren't nearly as entertaining as those portrayed in *Rain Man*, nor are they quite the drain on me that they were for Tom Cruise's Charlie. I enjoy them; Kim *loves* them. Besides taking us back and forth across the U.S. to deliver Kim's message, they keep us in a steady supply of anecdotes, both hilarious and heartrending.

One of the most comical of these everyday episodes came just before we hit the road one morning. (Of course, you would have had to have been there to capture the full effect of what I call Kim's "absent-minded professor syndrome.")

Kim and I had just showered at a motel and I had stepped out of the enclosure to dry myself off. I handed Kim a towel to do the same. He was still standing in the tub patting himself dry when I left the bathroom. Then "Dad, Dad!" he screamed. "Come fast! The bathtub's sinking!"

I rushed back inside the room, and there stood Kim, still inside the tub, clutching a shower bar (complete with curtain) and hoisting it over his head as if he were a weightlifter. "All of a sudden the bathtub started to sink," he howled. Then, his look of terror gradually fading as he realized that the bar had merely come loose in his hands, he flashed a sheepish grin.

I reached up and took hold of the bar while he stepped out onto the tile floor, asking, "Will the tub leak, Dad?"

I had him watch as I bent the ends of the bar back into their wall brackets. Now Kim was all smiles. "Thanks, Dad. I was almost in the Olympics, wasn't I?"

You Don't Mock America!

A GOSSIP WAS COMPLAINING ABOUT HER NEIGHBOR TO A visiting friend. Her neighbor was so dirty, it was a disgrace to the neighborhood. "Just look, those clothes she has on the line and sheets and pillowcases all have black streaks up and down them."

Her guest replied, "It appears, my dear, that the clothes are clean; the streaks you see are on your windows."

Seeing as how I served in World War II as an Air Force photographer/gunner, I guess over the years I've unwittingly passed my patriotic sentiments on to my son:

> August 10, 1991. Roseanne Barr had been widely criticized in the media for her screaming and rude rendition of "The Star Spangled Banner" prior to a San Diego Padres baseball game. While driving Kim to work, I remarked on how sacred the national anthem was to me and that I didn't approve of anyone desecrating it. In almost the same breath, I mentioned that neither could I tolerate disrespect for our flag.
>
> Kim's response demonstrated that he shared my views. "What should we do about 'Barr's strangled banner'?" he asked disgustedly. "She's from Utah, you know. Maybe she forgot to grow up while she was in school."

Sometimes You Oughtn't Ask

K IM'S HUNDREDS OF PRESENTATIONS OVER THE PAST
seven years have yielded more than a few
embarrassingly touchy moments:

> Kim was zigzagging across the church hall carrying a
> microphone so that the audience could hear
> the questions being asked as well as his
> responses. For the last few minutes he had
> been taking people's birth dates and making
> his usual calculations.

KimKwip—
Watching several
sparrows eating bread
crumbs outside the
window: "Why don't
those little birds ever
grow into big birds?"

> An elderly gentleman, his head bowed,
> his eyes cast down chestward and his body
> shaking noticeably from a palsy condition,
> was settled into an aisle seat. Spotting the
> man, Kim made his way over to him and asked, "What day
> were you born, sir?" A woman seated next to the
> gentleman (presumably his daughter) kindly answered that
> he was born on April 13, 1901. "Good Friday!" exclaimed
> Kim. "You will be 90 this year!"
>
> I stepped over to his microphone and prodded for more
> information. "Since 1901, what years has his birthday
> fallen on Good Friday?"
>
> Kim quickly ticked off six or seven years and told the
> man that he was a fine person. Following up on this
> response, I then asked, "When will his next birthday come
> on Good Friday?"
>
> Kim softly patted the somewhat dazed man on the head
> and quietly said, "Sir, I don't think you will make it—2007."
>
> Since then, I don't ask those kinds of questions.

"Meet My Aunt Phyllis!"

K IM ENJOYS BEING AT THE FOREFRONT OF PROMOTING The Arc (with its continuum of services to assist the handicapped in job training and placement, living skills, etc.), spreading understanding and goodwill, and nourishing individual potential—"worthy" goals, indeed. But, alone, Kim's message could never have reached so many.

Kim's support team is rounded out by two lovely ladies, who share and strengthen his goals:

> This night the questions centered mostly around small towns and cities. A person gives Kim the name of a city, anywhere in the world, and Kim then identifies the location of the city, the highways running out of it, the area code, the general ZIP code, usually something of historical interest about the area, what phone company the person pays her bill to, and the TV stations received in that locale.
>
> A young man raised his hand and asked, "Do you know the name of the great man who was born in Antimony?" (Antimony is a small town in southern Utah).
>
> Kim, unable to suppress a smile, cocked his head to the side, handed me the microphone and worked his way down the aisle towards a brightly dressed, curly-haired woman seated on the front row of the chapel. "He was married to my Aunt Phyllis!" he announced, putting his hand on the woman's shoulder. (Phyllis's husband had passed away a couple of years previously, so we invite her to accompany us to Kim's presentations as often as she's able.)
>
> Aunt Phyllis pulled herself up from her seat as the two hugged one another. Then Kim turned to the audience and added, almost as an afterthought, "And *another* important man from Antimony was Philo T. Farnsworth, who invented television."
>
> A look of pride, accompanied by a couple of happy tears, came across Aunt Phyllis's face. Mine, too. Kim knew who was most important to *him*.

Kim, Alison, and Brian grew up being loved by Aunt Phyllis, 1957

A Dearer Friend You'll Never Find

B ECOME A POSSIBILITARIAN," URGED NORMAN VINCENT
Peale. "No matter how dark things seem to be or actually
are, raise your sights and see possibilities—always see them,
for they're always there."

Well, I don't know anyone who better exemplifies
optimism and seeing the possibilities in obstacles than our
friend Mary Ruth. You can't easily miss her—and you won't
easily forget her!

Her hair is honey-blonde, permed in a Margaret Thatcher-
like bouffant. She's a meticulously dressed woman, about five
feet, five inches tall, and will inevitably be visiting with
everyone within sight. In her early seventies, she is a great-
grandmother three times over. And if you look closely at her
smile, you will see the glint of a shiny gold tooth, which
sometimes twinkles as she speaks to you in her occasional
Tennessee drawl.

Mary Ruth "Gold Tooth" Haslam, 1987

Her name is Mary Ruth Haslam. But to Kim she is "Mary Ruth with the Gold Tooth"—a special friend with lots of love to spare.

For the last 13 years of my work at the Utah State Office of Education as its Public Information Officer and Marketing Specialist, this grand lady, who was my executive secretary and total supporter, became an important part of our lives. She is the kind of friend who only comes along once in a lifetime.

When Kim, in 1979, became my primary responsibility, this lady provided immeasurable encouragement and assistance to both Kim and me. She had undergone a divorce several years earlier. Still, she possessed an uncanny knack for bringing smiles to others. Her pat answer to "And how are you today, Mary Ruth?" would be, "Just happy . . . and you?"

KimKwip—After carefully crossing the street to our home upon exiting the bus: "I waited for 16 cars to go by before I started across. Cars don't pay much attention to other people, do they?"

When the excitement over the reality of the movie *Rain Man* began to materialize, Mary Ruth became a regular attendee at Kim's presentations. And as Kim began to move further into the "celebrity spotlight," she was always there to help.

Our biggest booster retired from the State Office of Education a couple of years before I did. Today, as a great-grandmother and a woman busy serving most anyone who needs help, she is an integral member of our team.

With Mary Ruth's Margaret Thatcher-style hairdo and our English neighbor Muriel's accent, we frequently hear Kim comment, "Mary Ruth, you look like her, but Muriel talks like her!"

Countless friends and acquaintances have asked us why Mary Ruth and I don't marry; we attend all sorts of social events together (some alone, without Kim)—it would be a perfect match. But she understands that my first priority is caring for Kim. I could not jeopardize that responsibility by forming any other intimate relationship. Besides, leaving things as they are at present, she can enjoy her independence, and I, mine.

Yet, her devoted companionship is also very important to me. A born-again Christian, a dedicated, unselfish follower of Jesus Christ, she is always more than pleased to offer assistance. She's like a godmother and a true friend to Kim in every way, and Kim feels and understands her deep love for him:

> *KimKwip—As we motored down the highway, the on-the-hour news was about to come on. Kim punched in a stereo cassette and turned off the radio, murmuring, "It isn't the news I don't like to listen to, it's what they report on it."*

Mary Ruth owns a light blue Chrysler-made car with a license plate that has three numbers followed by the letters DEF. She also volunteers as a secretary at the Utah Blind Center.

As one day we pulled into her driveway and stopped just behind her parked car, Kim squinted through our windshield at her license plate and asked, "Dad, why would Mary Ruth choose those letters when she works with blind people?"

Kim, in a rare use of imagery, enthusiastically tags our little quartet consisting of Aunt Phyllis, Mary Ruth, and the two of us: "Three old apples and one young apple hanging on the same tree! You know that's the way it is, Mary Ruth with the gold tooth."

Family and Friends—Anchoring Kim's Life

ALONG WITH HIS BELOVED BOOKS AND MUSIC, FAMILY AND friends are still Kim's primary anchor. First and foremost is his mother, Jeanne. Though busily involved in her own married life with her husband, she is always ready and willing to care for Kim whenever I am unable to take him with me. His brother, Brian, and his sister, Alison—who, I'm sorry to have discovered so late, were forced to grow up in an environment that by necessity usually catered to the needs of their disabled brother—are also intensely concerned about his welfare. They dearly love him and are "right there" whenever they're needed.

Every family member—including uncles, aunts, and cousins—as well as some very special friends like Carol (who passed away in late 1994) and Jim Jensen, Jean Pugmire, Joan Bowden, Art and Bonnie Jackson, Oral Ballam, Daimar Robinson, Helen Holt, Bud Bowman, and dozens more have repeatedly demonstrated their attachment to and love for Kim.

He Does *Exactly* As He's Told

WITH SO MANY LOVED ONES TO ENCOURAGE HIM, KIM has gone from shutting off human interactions to where now he's a keen observer of them—a real student of human nature.

But over and over his literal mind will take control when he finds himself in a spellbound world filled with all sorts of people:

> We were seated in one of our favorite restaurants, looking over the menu and waiting for our hostess to take our order. Again it was during the time of Desert Storm, and Kim was talking up a storm about Saddam and the plight of the people in Kuwait. Because my hearing has deteriorated over the years, Kim is in the habit of speaking a bit louder to me, especially when we're in the shower or riding in the car. And on this occasion he was making sure I could hear him.
>
> As Kim jabbered on about "Dam Saddam," every now and again diners at the tables near us would glance up from their meals. Most were eavesdropping; one or two, however, were clearly annoyed at Kim's piercing voice.
>
> I leaned over to him and said, "Kim, you need to talk more quietly. You need to lower your voice."
>
> He looked at me with a puzzled expression—pondering the meaning of my words. Then, very slowly, he slid off his seat and down under the table—literally, "lowering his voice."

"It's Your Question—You Answer It"

KIM'S UNIQUE BRAIN STRUCTURE HAS DEPRIVED HIM OF much of his proficiency for analytical thought. Facts come to him easily, concepts are impossible. To quote from Dr. Christensen: "He can rattle through the presidents of the United States quicker than most people could read them. But to take what may be more important than who's been president and talk about what is a democracy, what does that mean to us, then Kim begins to stumble."

For this reason Kim seldom voices philosophical statements—nor does he clarify those he does utter. I'm not

even sure he has the ability to deliberate on that kind of
thinking. But now and then something will spill out of his
mouth that is highly thought-provoking and up for
interpretation.

Some of Kim's best one-liners surface when his target is a
person who insists on plying sarcasm or who otherwise seems
menacing:

> We were standing before an audience of educators and
> special educators at the University of Texas. The questions
> thrown out had been a mix of personal items directed
> towards me with a broad assortment of intellectual
> inquiries directed towards Kim.
>
> One individual, a male teacher who seemed a bit
> negative in his body language as Kim responded to
> comments from others, raised his hand and asked, "If you
> are so smart, Kim, maybe you can tell us which came first:
> the chicken or the egg?"
>
> Without a second's hesitation, Kim shot back in an
> unusually feisty tone, "Did you ever see an egg cross the
> road?"
>
> A few minutes later, after Kim had recited several lines

from Shakespeare, the same individual again raised his hand. This time Kim, a bit perturbed and warily eyeing the aggressor, moved down into the audience as the question was asked: "You seem to know a lot of verse. Maybe you can tell me who said, 'Bury me not on the lone prairie?'"

Kim took the man's hands in his own, pulled him to a standing position and cried out, "You did, sir!"—then, to enormous applause and laughter, gently eased him back down into his chair.

When Kim is badgered or feels threatened he can adopt a rather firm approach. In such instances, he is by nature both 100 percent truthful but also 100 percent humane. He seldom tries to put anybody down (though at times he's been known to deflect—verbally, of course—any form of rudeness).

There was one time, though, when he came as close as I've ever seen him to telling a fib in order to strike fear in his antagonist:

> We were out for a casual stroll on the sidewalk running through one of the greens that separate the condominiums where we live, when suddenly a young man on roller blades came racing around the corner, straight towards us. I quickly moved off the walkway as the youngster hurdled past. Kim, however, was not as easily moved. Holding his ground as the teen shot by, he shouted, "You are not allowed to skate on the greens!"
>
> The youth skidded to a stop, turned around, and approached us, his arms folded across his chest. "Who says so?" he muttered under his breath.
>
> Kim glanced up at me as if to say, "What'll we do now?" Then he pointed in the opposite direction and replied matter-of-factly, "That cop at the end of the walk"—a quick-thinking comeback that sent the hapless skater disappearing from sight back down the walk from where he had come.

Telling It Like It Is

S O THE STORY GOES, A GENTLEMAN, SEEING A BLIND woman standing on a busy street corner waiting for someone to help her cross the intersection, stepped up to her and asked, "May I go across with you?"

Well, I'm afraid Kim at present isn't quite so genteel in his dealings with people, but he's trying. Still, he tends to tell it like it is:

> It was at a Rotary Club meeting in St. Louis where one of the members was trying to cajole Kim. As I've mentioned, Kim doesn't take well to teasing or joking; you have to play it pretty straight or he might decide to ignore you completely.
>
> "Who invented the left-hand screwdriver?" the fellow demanded.
>
> Kim, feeling he was being patronized, ignored the question and surveyed the audience in search of another raised hand. But the man didn't take the hint. "You don't know who invented the left-hand screwdriver?" he repeated, a little louder this time.
>
> Kim, challenged, bristled slightly, then climbed down off the elevated platform. Swiveling his head from side to side, he made his way over to where the man was sitting and said, "You always try to be funny? What is your job? How did you get into the Rotary Club?"
>
> The fellow was obviously embarrassed at having been singled out. "I was just kidding with you," he squirmed. "My job? I'm in the insurance business. I work for one of the largest insurance companies in America."
>
> After staring down at him for a moment, Kim offered some advice: "Maybe you should change your job. Why don't you start your own business and then try to mind it."

A Nobel Prize-Winner's "Hairing Aid"

THE TRITE BUT TRUE PLATITUDE "PLEASE BE PATIENT . . .
God isn't finished with me yet," applies to all of us. No
matter how old or young, rich or poor, each of us has within
us a gold mine of potential just waiting to be tapped.
Likewise, each of us, in a sense, is still feeling our way along
life's road, struggling to find out who we are.

The same goes for Kim. Every day he's hard at work
cultivating and adorning his personal garden, a plot filled
with both weeds (obstacles or opportunities, depending how
you look at them) and blossoms (skills and character traits).
And at times a weed pops up that might yet evolve into a
beautiful flower:

> One of our English relatives had sent us a news clipping
> from Norwich announcing a grandchild's upcoming
> wedding. On the back side of the article was a short article
> about a Nobel Prize being awarded to a researcher in
> radiology, Dr. Rosalind Yallow. Kim, of course, was more
> interested in the clipping's back side.
>
> Several months later, Dr. Yallow accepted an invitation
> to speak at a nearby university. Kim wasn't all that
> interested in hearing her scientific opinions, but he wanted
> to meet her so he could tell her how he had heard about
> her special honor. So we attended the event.
>
> After the meeting had ended and most of the people
> had left the room except for Dr. Yallow and several of her
> peers, Kim walked up to her. She acknowledged him and
> extended her hand, which he promptly took in his.
>
> "You are a special lady, Rosalind," he declared in a
> sincere voice. My first thought was that Kim's heartfelt
> remark sounded extraordinarily sincere, especially coming
> from him. Then his next comment—one spoken out of
> unfeigned curiosity, in a voice that all those present
> couldn't help but hear—brought me back to reality: "How
> does a 63-year-old woman keep her hair so black?" With

her entourage of professors and doctors looking on in stunned silence, Dr. Yallow, her eyes tearing up in delight, countered, "I dye it!"

When the laughter brought on by Kim's innocent query and Dr. Yallow's good-natured retort had subsided, Kim showed her the clipping, gave her a long hug, and thanked her for being "a fine person" and "a woman of history."

His Mission: To Touch, to Connect

KIM HAS TOUCHED MANY LIVES, BOTH LITERALLY AND figuratively. He shakes hands, he hugs, he sometimes rubs noses with new friends. He wants to make them feel good and for them to like him.

However, he's never afraid to stand up for what he believes:

> One of Kim's first occasions to mingle with people outside the Utah area took place in Charlotte, North Carolina, where we traveled to help raise funds for The Arc of Charlotte and to boost awareness of people with special abilities. The evening before the fund-raiser event, Kim had been a guest of several television sports broadcasters.
>
> About 7:30 the next morning, the phone rang in our hotel room. It was the president of the Charlotte United Way. She had seen Kim on TV the night before and asked if his schedule would permit him to meet that day with the United Way at their final report noon luncheon. We were able to reschedule a couple of appointments and joined the nearly 300 volunteers at noon.
>
> After we had eaten, one of the United Way officers brought a microphone to Kim and invited his comments. Kim first thanked the volunteers for all the work they had done to raise money to help people in need, and he made special

KimKwip—Asked during a presentation if he had any siblings: "I have a sister you know only by respect."

Kim, Brian, and Alison, in the good old days, 1958

mention of those who worked at United Way day care centers serving preschoolers with disabilities.

Then with his right hand still clutching the mike, Kim reached for his beverage with his left hand. Raising it to his lips, he asked, "What is this we're drinking?" A woman across the table from him said everyone was drinking iced tea—always the preferred beverage at Southern meals.

Kim lifted the glass higher until it reached eye level and spoke loudly into the microphone: "'Thou shalt not taint my body,' said the prophet Joseph Smith, Article 89 of the Doctrine and Covenants, Church of Jesus Christ of Latter-day Saints." The audience laughed and applauded, with few understanding what he was talking about.

Immediately following his remarks, I took him outside to be interviewed by a local TV reporter. Leaving him with the reporter and his cameraman, I went back inside the building to collect a few guests who had come with us to the luncheon.

About 20 minutes later, I located Kim, still talking to the reporter, but now sitting on the lawn in front of him. The cameraman was nowhere to be seen.

"Anything wrong?" I asked the reporter.

"Not really," he replied. Then he explained the

circumstances that led up to their follow-up chat: "I was just finishing up the interview when he reached up, put his hands on top of my head and began to sing the song from *Rain Man* about 'the head bone's connected to the neck bone, the neck bone's connected to the shoulder bone,' and so on. Then he gradually moved down my body as he sang. Just singing and laughing the whole time. Finally, I just sat down on the ground and he started to tell me about the movie and that particular song."

"Did you get an interview?" I asked, apologizing if Kim had been a problem. "And could I see the video?"

"Oh, he was just fine," shrugged the reporter. "No real problem at all —but I already had to send the tape into the studio with my cameraman. It might need some editing before it airs in a couple of hours."

I thanked him, and he assured me that the show would be an interesting, albeit unusual, program. We later found a television set and sat down to watch the exchange between Kim and the reporter.

The interview opened with clips of Kim on the previous night's sport show. Then it cut to the reporter outside the building where we had eaten lunch. "How did you feel about your visit with the United Way of Charlotte today?" asked the reporter.

"They are great people. They work hard to help others. I liked them a lot!" Kim began. I smiled and nodded in agreement. Then the bomb dropped. "But you know," he continued, his voice rising in alarm, "they tried to poison me!"

The interview quickly cut from Kim to another, live, in-station newsman. This anchor, who was also a member of the bishopric of one of Charlotte's LDS (Mormon) congregations, explained that in the Mormon religion there is a code of values, or a principle, called the "Word of Wisdom," counsel found in the 89th section of one of the church's four books of

KimKwip—While attending a July 4th church breakfast, one elderly gentleman had his plate stacked with pancakes. Kim stared at the heaping plate, then at him, and said, "Some people always eat a lot when it's free."

scripture, the Doctrine and Covenants.

The Word of Wisdom, he went on to inform his listeners, is a health code advising Mormons that, among other things, it is harmful for them and unacceptable to the church to partake of alcohol, tobacco, coffee or tea. At the luncheon, Kim had been served a glass of iced tea, which had prompted his comment about being poisoned. The interview concluded with Kim chatting with a group assembled around the reporter.

Several weeks after returning home to Salt Lake, we received a letter from the First Presidency of the LDS Church complimenting Kim on his unique missionary work in Charlotte, where he helped teach nearly three million people about the many benefits of the Word of Wisdom.

Adding Practicality to a Metaphor

HOW SMART IS KIM? THE QUESTION IS ASKED AT LEAST once a week, usually during a time when Kim is off pacing the room or auditorium, fidgeting in a corner, or busy fiddling with his fingers.

Well, I'm not sure, but I do know that he gets smarter every day. I'm also convinced that there are different kinds of "smart," and while for some, dribbling and passing a basketball may come easily, for others the athletic skill may be beyond their ability to master. And so it is with other aptitudes: one's gift may lie in artistic or musical pursuits; another may excel in math, logic, or science; yet another will discover she has a knack for getting along with people, or for communicating effectively, or for managing money. The quasi-"Gumpism" *Smart is as smart does* is not only a cliche, it's a truism:

In the mid-1980s, at the request of Dr. Jean Pugmire,

emeritus professor from Utah State University, a psychology team from Stanford University visited USU in Logan, Utah, to give Kim a battery of intelligence tests. The information they gathered would be used to analyze Kim's intellectual activities in a series of brain conferences held for students studying education at the university.

The results were extremely interesting to the professionals—but quite disheartening to me. His I.Q. was calculated to be 74, the area in which most mentally retarded individuals score.

When we discussed the specifics of the testing, one of the psychologists expressed his opinion that this grade (74) was not indicative of Kim's true intelligence. Rather, it better represented his inability to cope with abstract thinking. His interpretations of and answers to questions relating to metaphors and to math problems were, to say the least, atypical. His responses simply did not conform to the expectations of the testing evaluations.

The results of the studies also placed Kim's reasoning level at about 88 percent. Why? Kim apparently had taken every word and expression from the tests as being literal in every way.

As time passed, and Kim became a "part of the world" and was talking to and with hundreds of people everywhere, it became evident to me that his projected I.Q. was an inadequate measure of what his brain contained and could accomplish. In fact, as his personality became better understood (primarily by myself and by several close friends who were involved in monitoring his presentations and capabilities), a definite quality surfaced from deep within him: He was so totally honest that practical, absolute answers and applications governed every facet of his reasoning. His mind, similar to a computer's hardware, can only perceive reality, hard fact.

As Kim has emerged from his introverted shell, I've taken the time to review some of the "abstract" questions Kim was unable to properly evaluate and answer during his I.Q. testing. For instance, one question read: What do you think is meant by the statement: "A rolling stone gathers no moss"?

As are all his responses to such metaphors, Kim's verbal reply was very practical: "If you learn to sing good, that green stuff will grow all over you!"—in effect, a real compliment to the singing group The Rolling Stones, but a no-score on his tests.

Some three years after the Stanford tests were performed, several psychologists decided to reevaluate Kim's mental capabilities. Their conclusion: Considering the uniqueness of Kim's learning abilities, his inventory of information and his inability to weigh most abstract information, his "Knowledge Quotient" (substituted for the normal I.Q. identification) is in the realm of 184, plus or minus five points.

KimKwip—To former U.S. First Lady Rosalyn Carter, an advocate for the needs of children and persons with disabilities: "Your husband is a good peanut."

Spending, as I do, the majority of my 24 hours a day with Kim, observing him at home and with audiences, and witnessing the mind-boggling volume of facts he calls upon to answer nearly any question in numerous subject areas, my understanding of the power of the human brain substantiates the 184 K.Q.

Still, in all my dealings with Kim, I say with certainty that his heart is infinitely bigger than his brain.

Questions and Answers—Plus More Metaphors

ONE OF THE MOVIE *RAIN MAN*'S LIGHTER MOMENTS IS when Raymond wanders off by himself and tries to cross at an intersection. Halfway across he glances up and sees the flashing DON'T WALK sign. Immediately obeying the command, he stops in the middle of the street, snarling traffic for several minutes.

With Kim, such an incident could conceivably happen.

The same goes for his presentations—facts reign supreme. When Kim is asked a direct question, one which has a definite answer, he steps right up and answers it. But when a question is worded so as to nuzzle up against his more vulnerable, private self, he will more likely serve up an adjacent answer, thus sidestepping controversy. Suddenly his mind begins running in concentric circles,

> *KimKwip—*
> *Sitting next to*
> *me at church:*
> *"Why does that*
> *baby keep*
> *crying? Is it in*
> *trouble with its*
> *mom?"*

searching for symmetry. It's amazing how quickly his mind can distinguish between the two types of questions.

From Kim's responses to common expressions, I've been able to come up with what I call a "Metaphors: Now You Know What They Really Mean" list:

> What does the metaphor "Don't count your chickens before they hatch" mean?
> Kim's interpretation: "Use a cacklelator to know how many chickens there are."

> Metaphor: Follow in your father's footsteps.
> Kim: "Hold Dad's arm so you won't get lost in the airport."

> Metaphor: Be sure to smell the flowers!
> Kim: "A Dristan a day keeps the pollen away."

> Metaphor: Never change horses in midstream.
> Kim: "Only ride your horse on a houseboat."

> Metaphor: A bird in the hand is worth two in a bush.
> Kim: "Admiral Byrd was never invited to the White House to meet Barbara and George."

> Metaphor: Hope springs eternal.
> Kim: "Because he made so many servicemen and women laugh." (referring to Bob Hope)

Metaphor: People who live in glass houses
  shouldn't throw stones.
Kim: "Don't throw a rock at your cat when
  you let it out of the house."

Metaphor: Believe with all your heart.
Kim: "You might need a part of a transplant
  to do it."

Metaphor: In God we trust.
Kim: "Save it now so you can pay it later."

Metaphor: Never cry wolf.
Kim: "Don't try to bark your head off."

Metaphor: What is meant by the Golden Rule?
Kim: "Do it! But do it to yourself first."

Metaphor: Look before you leap.
Kim: "Aim right at the Budweiser truck's license plate.
  Yahoo!" (referring to the beer commercial starring
    the three frogs)

Sing Me a Few Bars, Ms. Metro

AMONG KIM'S MOST RARE GIFTS IS HIS PENCHANT FOR music—all kinds of music. He can name and sing almost any hit from the war years. He'll even tell you who made the song popular and the band that first recorded it.

He revels in singing the hits of Elvis and the Beatles, even frequently drawing upon the popular sounds of the '70s, '80s, and '90s. His energetic songs often bring screams of delight from his junior and senior high school audiences.

But, give him an opera or a selection of purely classical music, and any worries he might have evaporate in an aura of transcending peace. His booming voice vibrates in ecstasy with the music.

Much of Kim's love of the classics stems from his early childhood, listening to his mother play records on the phonograph. He would hear them only once, then sit down and study the record label and read the information on the jacket cover. Album by album he came to learn much about the musical greats of yesteryear. Even now he remembers and willingly shares the music and the details surrounding it, including the order of each piece on the record:

From the late '70s up until today, Kim has cherished the friendship of another music lover, a grand woman who has helped introduce him to the Saturday radio broadcasts of the New York Metropolitan Opera. She provides him with schedules and news articles about the works and their composers. After studying them, he usually calls her on the telephone, challenging her to discover the links his mind is making between operatic themes, composers' lives, historical dates, and current events. They also enjoy humming back and forth over the phone to each other the melodies they know and love so well.

Daimar Robinson is a highly intelligent person and a talented writer. For years she wrote magazine reviews on local symphony and operatic events. Kim reads every article Daimar sends him, then "gets on the horn" for their spirited discussions.

While before he seldom listened to the radio for any extended period, Daimar patiently encouraged him to learn how to turn on his radio and locate his favorite broadcasts (though for a number of years he never could remember to turn down the volume). Through her continual rapport and encouragement, Kim has learned how to tune in KUER-FM, one of Utah's classical radio stations. And when we travel the state by car, he eagerly scans the dial to locate the FM stations in every locale, still especially enjoying the Metropolitan Opera broadcasts.

Daimar is an inspiration to his love of great music and is one of his very special friends. Thank you, Daimar.

Water, Water Everywhere!

L EONARDO DA VINCI, THE STORY IS TOLD, WAS WORKING feverishly on his masterpiece "The Last Supper," when he became angry with a certain man and lost his temper with him, lashing out with bitter threats. When he returned to his canvas, da Vinci attempted to recommence his work but found himself unable to do so. First, he had to lay down his tools and search for the man to ask his forgiveness. The man accepted his apology and Leonardo returned to his workshop—to finish painting the face of Jesus.

At times Kim, like anybody, becomes anxious or upset. But he hardly if ever loses his temper (though at times I wouldn't blame him if he did; a good tantrum once in a while is a good release for pent-up emotions). He remains composed, patient to the end. That is, for the most part:

Kim's aunt and uncle, Claire and Terry Peek, were visiting us in Salt Lake. One night we decided to treat them to dinner. We chose a relatively new yet highly recommended Vietnamese restaurant in South Salt Lake.

The manager graciously welcomed our party of ten and seated us at a long table filled with place settings and stunning flower arrangements. After looking over the menu and ordering a hodgepodge of delicacies, we chatted until the first course arrived.

The manager, who also was one of our servers, was trying to set down one of the steaming food platters, when he accidentally tipped over Kim's ice water—a torrent which promptly spilled onto Kim's lap.

Kim instantly thrust back his chair and came to his feet. Then he released his belt and let his sopping pants drop to the floor. Other guests starred in disbelief as Kim shuffled about, shrieking, "Dad, the boat people are trying to drown me!"

An apologetic manager, unable to understand what Kim was saying but comprehending all too clearly his obvious distress, hurriedly toweled the puddle of water from Kim's chair as we rushed to pull his trousers up and calm him down.

On the whole, it was a great—and most memorable—evening. Both the food and the friendship were outstanding. So, if you ever find yourself in Salt Lake and the urge for a delicious Vietnamese meal hits you, just call Kim or me to find out the location of this fine restaurant. (However, you might want to bring along your beach attire!)

> *KimKwip*—
> Commenting on
> a TV celebrity he
> had just met:
> "She's a pretty
> lady except her
> shoes are always
> too tight."

The World's Best-Loved Oscar

TWO YEARS AFTER BARRY MORROW ACCEPTED THE OSCAR for his screenplay, we drove to California to see him and his family. It was a great reunion. Since our last visit, he had moved into new offices just north of his home in Claremont, and so he invited us to take a tour.

Several awards were displayed on the walls; books and trophies highlighted the main room. And high up on one of the shelves stood the golden Oscar. We hadn't seen it since the morning after the Academy Award show when we stopped by Barry's home to meet with the media and to congratulate Barry personally.

Barry invited us to sit down. Then, smiling, he reached up, gently lifted the statuette down, and held it at arm's length. You could see the light dancing in his eyes as his thoughts drifted back to that special evening two years earlier.

"Beautiful, isn't it?" he said. "I wouldn't have it if it weren't for you, Kim. It belongs to both of us. I want to share it with you. OK?"

"You can't do that, Barry," I protested. "It's such an important monument to your talents. It needs to be near you and your friends."

Barry shook his head. "No, I really want Kim to take it home with him. Keep it for a couple of years. Enjoy it. Share it with your friends, too."

He picked up a flight bag from his desk, tucked the statue into it, and handed it to me. Then he hugged me very emotionally. I returned the gesture. Next he approached Kim, gave him a squeeze, and said, "We are a great team!"

Kim appeared overwhelmed—which doesn't happen very often! "Together," he began, measuring his words (another thing he isn't noted for!) and tilting his head forward and to one side, "We are forever, Barry." Then he turned away.

For a while we discussed with Barry just how we might best use the Oscar. "Share it with people," he told us, "just like you are sharing Kim with them. Then, when you feel you want to bring it back to me, we'll put it back on the shelf."

And share it we did!

During the ensuing two years, "Oscar" was our companion at nearly every presentation. We introduced it to those in attendance and let them hold it. They were thrilled, anxious, and most appreciative to Barry for making it all happen. Everyone of the more than 185,000 people who have handled it has treated it with reverence, stroking the smooth coldness of its legs and head. Transferred from hand to hand, over time much of the gold plating was entirely worn off.

At last it was time for the "real Oscar" to return to Barry, so I phoned to inform him that we were coming to California. I also told him of the great impact the statue had had in the lives of many and that I had made arrangements

Kim with "Oscar," 1992

with a jewelry company to restore the gold plating to its original state.

But Barry would have none of it. "I want it just the way it is. I want to be able to tell people that it has been the most shared and loved Oscar ever. That 185,000 people have had an opportunity to spend a few moments in its fantasy world." Then he added, "I might even think about making a movie about what's happened since *Rain Man* was released."

The Oscar holds so many memories for Kim and me, and for everyone who held it and admired what it represented. And for Barry, this symbol of excellence delivered a choice message to hundreds of thousands of people who share our planet: "You don't have to be a Rain Man to be different, because everybody is. Share . . . care . . . respect. Be the best you can be!"

A Blessing for All Seasons

A S NOTED, KIM'S "RELIGION" CONSISTS OF WHAT HE READS, sees, and hears, a patchwork of facts taken from novels, reference books, and histories. For him, reading a passage from the Bible and overhearing a question from a television game show probably carry the same weight. Deep religious reflection and analysis are beyond him.

But to say that Kim is "irreligious" would by the same token be untrue. Somehow, I believe the source of his spirituality—be it from his wealth of knowledge or from somewhere deep in his soul—is God:

> Because Kim is mentally disabled, it is not necessary for him to be baptized into the Mormon church. By decree, he is automatically a member. However, I decided that a "priesthood blessing" might give him a spiritual lift.
>
> So, following Kim's meeting with our local congregation one Sunday evening, he was invited to take a seat as I and a group of fellow elders, including several church authorities, encircled him and gently laid our hands upon his head. One of the elders began to pronounce the blessing and offer words of love and comfort, when suddenly Kim stood straight up.
>
> "Are we pressing too hard, Kim?" the elder asked. Kim stood very still, then looked around the room and said, "I have been thinking about becoming a member of the Church, but I don't think I can. I want to meet people of all faiths and be a part of their lives, too. I think I want to be a missionary just for God. I want to do whatever He thinks I ought to do for everyone."

KimKwip—
Discussing the Mormon philosophy of heaven— the three "Degrees of Glory" (Celestial Kingdom, Terrestrial Kingdom, and Telestial Kingdom) with the two home teachers who visit us each month: "My Dad and I have decided to go to the Cerebral Kingdom, but we'll invite you over."

One of the men tenderly threw his arm over Kim's shoulders and told him that what he said was very good. Then during the next few minutes, each member of the circle and others in the room came forward and warmly shook his hand.

Kim is truly a spiritual soul. He bears no malice or prejudice towards anyone, and his fondest wish is for all of us to be kind to one another.

God, I'm sure, is proud of him . . .

Your Visit with Kim Could Be Just Beginning

SOMEDAY YOU MIGHT RUN ACROSS SOMEONE PACING BACK and forth and mumbling to himself in the library. The person may not be Kim, but treat him with respect and kindness anyway.

But someday you really might run into Kim: in an airport, on a street corner, or he might be speaking at a school in your community. If not in person, you might read about him in the newspaper or see him on TV reminding everyone to respect others and to respect themselves. Or he might be visiting with a sportscaster about a piece of sports trivia or discussing history with a news team.

If you do run into him, just walk right up and say, "Hi, Kim!" I promise he'll take your hand, look you in the eye and say, "What's your name? ... Where are you from?"

Both you and he will be thrilled and amazed.

The journey's been fun!
Thank you for inviting us into your lives.

APPENDIX

O VERALL, HOW HAS THE MEDIA RESPONDED TO KIM? AND what influence have they had in how he and other individuals with disabilities are perceived? I've included in this appendix what I call Media Megabytes. For the interested reader, they recap a smattering of the hundreds of newspaper articles that have appeared over the past seven years. The sum of these reporters' writings together with the many examples and less partial viewpoints they offer may provide insight into who Kim is, why he does what he does, and how he operates in the frenzy of the public eye.

MEDIA MEGABYTES

KIM IS 1 IN 7 MILLION: AN EXTRAORDINARY SAVANT
by Lois M. Collins, The Deseret News,
Salt Lake City, Utah, Nov. 10, 1988

• . . . His speech is clear, but he jumps from subject to subject, confusing listeners by "giving you the predicate, but not the subject" . . .

• Kim is a contradiction, either the very best or among the worst at performing a variety of tasks . . . He is brilliant in a number of areas: music, history, geography, calendars, literature, sports, movies, current events, weather and numbers, all greatly enhanced by a photographic memory.

• I tell Kim I was raised in Idaho Falls, and he rattles off telephone prefixes. He tells me about main roads in the city, the television station's tower on 17th Street. On learning my birthday, he says I was born on a Monday (I knew that). My birthday in 2020 will also fall on a Monday (a quick look at a perpetual calendar later confirms it) . . . I cannot always follow the conversation, but there is no doubt in my mind that he could trace his mental transitions for me, if I could think fast enough to follow it.

• Just four years ago . . . doctors determined Kim is a savant, and not retarded. His brain hemispheres are fused together and into his brain stem. The result seems to be an extraordinarily large "data storage area," but his motor skills suffer a great deal because connections are cut off . . .

• Kim cannot screen out anything. He is stimulated by everything around him, so it is hard for him to concentrate on any one thing . . . Kim has developed tools to aid his concentration, and some of them are disconcerting if you don't know what he is doing. At home, he twists a piece of venetian blind rope to help him focus. He paces. He shakes his hands. Most often, though, he hums to block out all the thoughts running simultaneously through his mind . . .

• Kim himself sees nothing unusual in his ability. "He just assumes that everyone else knows everything he does," his father said . . .

• . . . The longer and more you know him, the fonder you become of him. You get past the things that are different to find the person of quality.

A SALT LAKE SAVANT POSSESSES
INCREDIBLE POWERS OF MEMORY
by Terry Orme, The Salt Lake Tribune,
Dec. 11, 1988

• The adjective "unique" is especially appropriate in Kim's case. Experts estimate that there is one savant in every seven million people, and a savant usually has but one or two areas of expertise . . . [So] he is one in about 70 million . . .

• [With a single brain hemisphere and no corpus callosum], the filtering system normal people have is not in Kim. He has to sustain everything he hears or sees. In doing so, he has been forced to develop storage areas which are unbelievable.

Kim can remember the liner notes on the back of classical record album jackets that he read when he was 3. He can read a paperback book in less than two hours and remember all he has read. When he and his father were at a performance of "King Lear" at the Utah Shakespearean Festival a few years ago, Kim stopped an actor mid-soliloquy to point out that he had transposed two quatrains . . .

GOOD TIMES FOR THE REAL 'RAIN MAN'
by Janet Ghent, The Tribune, Oakland, California, Dec. 14, 1988

• Sitting by the table in his room at the San Francisco Hilton is a young man from Salt Lake City, with thick glasses, floppy bangs, a pale-blue suede jacket and extremely soft hands . . .

• . . . During the last year, he has been speaking out and serving as an inspiration to the many developmentally disabled children and adults who were once told they would never amount to anything . . .

• Kim has encyclopedic factual knowledge, a 185 I.Q., and subnormal reasoning and motor ability . . .

• "Kim was always the one and only inspiration for me," said Morrow. "Dustin made it a point to meet with many autistic savants, but 'Rain Man' was always Kim to me and Kim was always 'Rain Man.'"

• There are key differences between Kim and 'Rain Man.' Kim, the oldest of three children, has never been institutionalized, nor is he afraid of flying. He also refuses to put his talents to gambling . . . (He can count cards quite well, however.)

KIM, THE SAVANT WHO CAME TO HOLLYWOOD
by Lawrence Christon, Los Angeles Times, Jan. 8, 1989

• Kim is one of those special people who is both mentally handicapped and capable of spectacular feats of knowledge.

•[Autistics] have a limited repertoire of gestures and interests, like Kim's staring at his fingers. They have a lot of distress over trivial changes in the environment, which they counter with an insistence on sameness...

• . . . [Dr.] Christensen likens Kim's knowledge to computer retention. "It excludes integrative thinking," he said, "or the ability to abstract. You can't ask Kim what it means to be a citizen in a democracy or to interpret the meaning of a proverb. He can't interpret his information. What he possesses isn't, strictly speaking, intelligence . . . [Still], he is beyond any savant I have ever heard of . . . He's a landmark to our ignorance."

• [Barry Morrow shared the following]: "Once in Reno I tried to get Kim to play 21, like in the movie. He refused. He said it wouldn't be fair. I said the casino system isn't fair; it's always geared against the gambler. 'That's their problem,' he said. He played a slot machine and won. I swear it's his electric aura that tripped the machine off. But he just took his cup of money and said, 'Let's do something else.'"

• "When I first came here . . . " Kim began to say. "You were born here," said Fran, disregarding Kim's mystical note.

Kim went on to talk about family associations going back to the turn of the century (family is crucial to Kim's way of thinking), and in the next hour or so his mind took dazzling turns of free association in which historical facts, images, names and anecdotes poured out like an endless series of jazz improvisations.

• Fran offered Kim a cough drop. Kim put it into his mouth. His face strained, then he cracked it with a sound that resembled a jawbone unhinging. "He's never learned to suck on a cough drop," Fran said with a covert smile. "That sound always gets people in a restaurant."

He related how he had carried Kim up and down flights of stairs for 14 years before Kim learned how to walk stairs on his own—at school. "I came in one day to get him. They said, 'Don't go up. Wait here.' He came walking down for the first time in his life. I just about died . . ."

KIM: 'AN ISLAND OF GENIUS IN
THE SEA OF THE MENTALLY HANDICAPPED'
by Joseph Walker, The Deseret News,
Jan. 30–31, 1989

• Shelley Thomas first met Kim about four years ago . . . The little man was probably more than 30 years old, and yet there was something childlike and harmless about him. He had the look of the mentally handicapped about him, but he spoke with intelligence—even brilliance . . .

• . . . He does complicated payroll computations in his mind, but falls apart when someone suggests a change in his routine. He can recite cast lists and lines of dialogue from any of the scores of books, movies and plays he's read or seen, but he can't explain . . . what they mean. He has a perpetual calendar in his head that allows him to identify any day or date in history or the future, but he can't figure out how to sharpen his pencil.

How does he do it? As far as Kim is concerned, it's simple. "I just know my savantism," he says.

• "Sometimes he's hard to keep up with," [Shelley] Thomas admitted. "The way his mind makes connections, you can be talking about one thing, he'll make some obscure association and the next thing you know he's a million miles away talking about something you had no intention of talking about . . .

"The family was hesitant to have any publicity, but they decided to trust me with this," Thomas said. "And Kim is just so full of love and trust. I didn't want to betray that . . . The joy of this project was just being around him—he's such a sweetheart . . . I hope that seeing him will help shatter the notion of what a mental handicap is. I know I will never look at anyone who is allegedly 'impaired' the same way again."

But beyond that, Thomas just wants people to care. "My hope is that people will fall in love with him like I did . . . "

'RAIN MAN' WRITER BARRY MORROW
SHARES HIS FASCINATION

HE WANTED TO TELL A TOUCHING STORY AFTER
MEETING UTAH 'MEGASAVANT'
by Chris Hicks, The Deseret News, Mar. 2, 1989

• "I was flabbergasted that such a human being could exist," [says Mr. Morrow]. "I'd read about people, and I'd spent much time in institutions and met autistic people with calendar skills, but I'd never met someone who could do it all."

• " . . . Now, perhaps, the real 'Rain Men' in the world will have a better time of having their plight understood, and maybe 'Rain Man' won't have to go away on the train next time."

REAL-LIFE 'RAIN MAN'
HAS AMAZING MENTAL POWERS—
BUT CAN'T SET A TABLE
TOUCHING STORY OF BIZARRE GENIUS WHO
INSPIRED OSCAR-WINNING FILM
The National Enquirer, Apr. 18, 1989

• "The character in the movie is an autistic savant," said his dad. "Children who are autistic are withdrawn, shy away from strangers and do not converse readily. My son is a savant (brilliant in some areas), but he is not autistic . . . He is a very warm, friendly, wonderful person . . .

"Even the scene in 'Rain Man' in which the savant character recites from a phone book is fictionalized. Kim doesn't read the alphabetical listings in the white pages—he memorizes the yellow pages. [Note: At that time—1989—he had switched over to the yellow pages; nowadays his inquiries are split pretty much down the middle between studying businesses and individuals.]

"When we visit a town where he's studied the telephone book he can point out stores which are new and which ones have gone out of business even though he's never been there before . . . "

RAIN MAN'S WORLD IS ALL IN HIS MIND
MEGASAVANT WHO INSPIRED FILM
WILL SPEAK IN CHARLOTTE
by Lawrence Toppman, The Charlotte Observer, Charlotte, N.C., Nov. 7, 1989

• If the size of our brains reflected the amount of knowledge stored in them, Kim Peek would need a hat as wide as the Astrodome.

Remember Raymond in "Rain Man," reading the phone book white pages for pleasure and reciting a waitress's phone number the next day? Kim can do that—he was a model for the character—though he prefers subjects found in the Yellow Pages. (He likes to read about gas stations and lighting stores and dry cleaners.)

• . . . Mention an opera he's heard, and he'll list principal characters—down to the least important, including the ranks of the soldiers—and hum arias and orchestral interludes.

How unique is he? When the *National Enquirer* profiled him in April, it didn't have to make up anything . . .

• For fun, Kim reads and goes to movies and reads and listens to music and reads and lectures and reads. In his spare time, he reads. He dines on a phone book and snacks on *TV Guide.*

He pores over newspapers the day after publication and never listens to newscasts. "Tragedies, particularly those involving children, upset him terribly," says Fran. "I think it's easier for him to deal with things if they're a little in the past.

"(Going outside the home) has been good for Kim. I wondered sometimes if I might have been exploiting him, because I thought having him appear before groups would be viewed that way. But after the first couple of questions, Kim is part of the group. It's almost a hypnotic, spiritual thing; he's so honest and innocent, that people sort of absorb him."

• Accounts describe Kim as shy, sweet, irascible when daily routines are altered, but physically affectionate. He likes to touch people in conversation, and he describes himself as "using the Dustin image"—gently touching foreheads with listeners he likes, as Hoffman did in "Rain Man."

He has a sense of humor, too, though you can't be sure when it's intentional. When a questioner asked which baseball player held the record for stolen bases at Brigham Young University, Kim replied, "I don't know. But I hope he gave them all back."

• " . . . He assumes everyone he meets has his powers of recall. If somebody doesn't keep up in a conversation, Kim assumes they're being polite and not interrupting," says Fran. "That's the amazing thing: He treats little kids and adults the same way. To Kim, everybody is his equal."

KIM PEEK: RAINMAN, MIRACLE MAN OR BOTH?
by M.J. Piaskowska, Star Tribune,
Casper, Wyoming, Mar. 21, 1993

• Kim's thinking process is difficult for the average person to follow. When asked a question, everything he's ever learned about the subject comes gushing out, not always in an order that the everyday person can understand. As his father explained, "He can't always give you a subject, but he will give you six or seven predicates. If you ask him to explain, his predicates line up."

• . . . Kim has no need to sightsee, his father added, because he already knows all about every place he visits.

When he's not working, lecturing or reading, Kim likes to relax by watching television. His favorite show is "Double Jeopardy." He found the simple "Jeopardy" show too boring, his father said. He also enjoys public television, especially "Masterpiece Theatre."

'20/20' LOOKS AT SAVANT'S LIFE
AFTER 'RAIN MAN'
by Harold Schindler, The Salt Lake Tribune,
Jan. 7, 1994

• . . . In Kim's case, his memory is, without exaggeration, incredible. His father, Fran Peek, recalls how Kim, the oldest of three [children], began reading at an early age and by 6 was absorbing volumes of the Book of Knowledge, because he could reach them from the lower shelf of the bookcase.

"My other two children would sit across the room and pick up a Dr. Seuss book, and Kim would sit on the other side of the room and recite the same book to them from memory!"

• His father explained that Kim's personality began to emerge. "It was amazing. He gained self-confidence. He was somebody, maybe a human being for a change."

For the first time in his life Kim found that adults wanted to speak to him and listen to him. [Bob] Brown, the *20/20* correspondent, called Kim Peek's emergence a small miracle. "He has come out to greet the world."

REAL-LIFE 'RAIN MAN' DAZZLES HUNDREDS
WITH MEMORY, WIT
by Joseph S. Stroud, Lexington Herald,
Lexington, Kentucky, Mar. 6, 1994

• "Do you know which book Poirot passed away in?" asked one woman after Peek boasted familiarity with Agatha Christie novels.

"The last one," Peek said, drawing laughter from the crowd. The pause gave him time to come up with *Curtain.*

• The purpose of Kim Peek's speeches, he said, was to urge people "to recognize and respect differences in others."

"So they could do what?" his father asked him.

"So they could be treated like other people, so we won't have any more problems in the world."

'MEGASAVANT' WHO WAS INSPIRATION FOR
AWARD-WINNING 'RAINMAN' FILM UNREELS
AMAZING FEATS OF MEMORY
by Michael Kashgarian,
Midland Reporter-Telegram, Midland, Texas,
Apr. 9, 1994

• . . . Peek made some associations Friday evening that
seemed to go beyond just recall. When answering some
questions, members of the audience seemed a bit confused at
the seemingly off-the-wall responses.

One young girl—instead of quizzing Peek about the day
of the week a certain date fell on or one of Mozart's
compositions—asked if the Midland Angels were going to
win the game that night.

As with some other responses, Peek burst into an
enthusiastic rendition of . . . a song.

One observant attendee recognized the song as "What's
the Buzz," from the play *Jesus Christ Superstar.* The song
relates Jesus' frustration on being asked by disciples and
others to predict the future . . .

• . . . An almost ever-smiling Peek appeared very
affectionate, hugging and holding hands with everyone who
asked a question.

The Arc Lightnewsletter
The Arc of Arizona, Inc., Summer 1994

• . . . [The Peeks'] audience expanded to millions recently
when ABC-TV's *20/20* traveled to Utah to meet them. The
segment was aired January 7 and the Peeks were besieged with
calls. Geraldo Rivera simply sent two first-class plane tickets
to the Peeks to get them on the show but Fran declined that

and other invitations from the tabloid talk shows. Their priority, he said, is to address events of The Arc and educational groups . . .

NOTED MEGA-SAVANT MAKES BIG HIT AT HALL
The Pro Football Hall of Fame INSIDER,
Summer, 1994

• . . . Kim recited a plethora of little-known facts about virtually every Hall of Fame member . . . as he toured the four-building complex . . . His rapid-fire dissertation when he spotted Doak Walker's jersey is a perfect example.

"Bobby Layne and Doak Walker played at Dallas Highland Park High School together. Layne went to the University of Texas and Walker to Southern Methodist. Bobby played in one Cotton Bowl and Doak played in two Cotton Bowls. They were drafted by different teams in the NFL. Layne by the Bears and Walker by the Lions. Did you know that?"

'RAIN MAN' VISITS HERE; LIFE WAS BASE FOR MOVIE
by Lance Coleman, Chattanooga Free Press,
June 10, 1994

• Megasavant Kim Peek met everyone at the door . . . with a hug for them and a nose-to-nose rub. He then asked their names and where they lived.

According to his father, [Kim] is now drastically different from the son he knew before the movie "Rain Man," which was based on his life.

"All we knew before was that he was quiet, alone, and read a lot," said Fran Peek. "Until he met (the film's screenwriter) Barry Morrow, everything was different . . . "

MAKE NO MISTAKE: KIM PEEK ISN'T THE 'RAIN MAN'

by Max McQueen, Tribune Newspapers,
Paducah, Kentucky, Sept. 10, 1994

• . . . When *Rain Man* became a huge global success, the Peeks suddenly found themselves living in a fish bowl. Hoffman encouraged Fran Peek to turn the "spotlight" around and use it to fuel positive attention for mentally-handicapped adults.

With that encouragement, Fran and Kim became a father-and-son team that visited local and regional associations for retarded citizens (ARC) . . .

• Kim was particularly moved by a sentence that a developmentally disabled gentleman at the Chandler/Gilbert ARC printed out for him. It read: "Everyone should know that we are all equally intelligent, just in different ways."

• Traveling and meeting people has been good for Kim. And his father, too. But it has its downside. Although they mean well, people—people like this reporter—want to make Kim into "Raymond." That person, as Fran Peek is quick to point out, is a "movie character." Kim is for real. Very real.

"I don't do the 'Rain Man' anymore," Kim said. "I'm just Kim."

'RAINMAN' TRIUMPHS USING SPECIAL ABILITIES

by Ruth Littman, The Detroit Jewish News,
Oct. 14, 1994

• . . . Ask him on which day of the week Halloween will fall in 1997, and he won't even take a fraction of a second to answer "Friday."

Quiz Kim on practically anything, and he'll tell you what's what. One woman at the JCC [Jewish Community Center] asked him what event coincided with her husband's birthdate of Feb. 20, 1938. Kim began reciting Adolf Hitler's Reichstag address . . .

• Together, [Kim and Fran] aim to change people's attitudes toward mental disabilities.

Disabled individuals should not be kept apart from the rest of society . . . [Says Fran]: "[Kim's] social skills have increased primarily because he's come out of a closet and into a world where people recognize him. People . . . pat him on the back and boost his self-esteem and confidence. This simply doesn't happen to a person who is kept in an institution . . ."

HIS DAY IN THE SUN
by Brian Geoghan, The York Dispatch, Nov. 11, 1994

• He squints, cocks his head, taps his right foot, pumps his left hand at his side. He sticks out his meaty bottom lip, then breaks into a wide-eyed grin. Through thick glasses, the megasavant finds eye contact necessary.

His disarming charm puts you at ease, even when he's in your face.

Kim Peek . . . has the proverbial steel trap between his ears . . . He has an insatiable appetite for information.

Peek can't do much with that information but devour it and share it with others. He's a megasavant, without peer in his capacity to retain facts.

But the same brain abnormality that gives Peek those mental abilities has stripped him of normal reasoning powers . . .

• Before "Rain Man," Peek led an introverted, private, safe life for 37 years. He rarely took risks and never left his father's side in public. Since the movie, he has evolved into a social bundle of energy . . .

As soon as he's in a room with people, he's gone from his father's wing, walking around the outer limits of the room, talking, singing, waiting for someone to engage him in conversation . . .

• As long as you ask questions, he'll chat. When the conversation slows for even a moment, he's off again, pacing the room, rapping his knuckles on the walls, talking and singing to himself, the hard look of concentration furrowed in his brow . . .

ORIGINAL 'RAIN MAN' TELLS HIS STORY IN YORK
by Christine Paskoski, The Evening Sun,
York, Pennsylvania, Nov. 11, 1994

• . . . He is very friendly, but easily becomes distracted. He will walk off abruptly in the midst of a conversation and sometimes bursts into song at odd times when something seemingly unrelated reminds him of a lyric or melody.

"He is kind of weaving two or three channels of thought at one time," Fran Peek explains.

REAL 'RAIN MAN' BRINGING GENIUS TO JACKSONVILLE
HUMAN 'KIM-PUTER' HELPING COUNCIL WITH
FREE APPEARANCE
by Bob Phelps, The Florida Times-Union,
Jacksonville, Florida, Feb. 21, 1995

• . . . Challenge him if you like. Ask for the zip code of your hometown, wherever it may be. He'll give the first three numbers with uncanny accuracy and tell you what the main route is into your town. Ask him what year Tchaikovsky finished the *Nutcracker Suite.* He'll not only tell you 1892 but sing several parts for you. Ask him the date of the Battle of Iwo Jima. He'll tell you that and the name of the Marine general who led it.

He tells it all in a foghorn voice punctuated by a deep chuckle . . .

• Peek sat on a bed at the Marina Hotel last night and rubbed his knees, slapped his hands together nervously, rocked back on the bed, paced around the room, and constantly chuckled to himself, enjoying interaction with visitors.

He answered a question accurately about the distance of Mars from the sun, about 130 million miles at its closest approach, then added, "Every 17 years, it gets closest to Earth, and that's when you have the best view."

In that fog-horn voice, he hummed several bars from Frederick Delius' *On Hearing The First Cuckoo,* noting the composer had lived for a short [time] in Jacksonville and talking about his home on the river here. "He lived from 1862 to 1934," Peek said . . .

• "Kim has no ability to retain memory of motor skills," his father said. For example, Kim forgets how to walk and thus exhibits the tentative steps in his walk that Dustin Hoffman portrayed so well in the movie. "Kim has to relearn how to brush his teeth every day," Fran Peek said.

•The difference *Rain Man* has made in his life was best described by Daniel Christensen at the University of Utah Medical Center in a telephone interview.

. Christensen . . . described how, when he first met Kim Peek 10 years ago, Peek hung his head and didn't speak. He faced a corner of Christensen's office while the doctor talked to the father. Christensen recalls: "When he left, I said, 'It was nice to meet you,' and he just said, 'Yes,' without looking at me and walked out."

A year ago, Christensen met Kim at a Rotary Club meeting in Salt Lake, and Peek hugged the doctor and said,

"'Nice to see you again, Dan,'

"That's how he has changed," the scientist said. "He's a very tender young man."

• The Peeks are not remotely as wealthy as the characters portrayed in *Rain Man* . . . Yet Fran Peek refuses to take money for their appearances. "We've traveled 64,000 miles and talked to 486,000 people since 1989," [he] said. "Honestly, we're doing it because Kim seems to enjoy it so much and it seems to do a lot of image-building for people like him . . ."

Fran Peek tells anyone who insists on donating something to send it to [a center for people with disabilities in their own community or to] the workshop at Columbus Community Center in Salt Lake where Kim Peek works . . .

Real 'Rain Man' urges students to be tolerant
by Joe Salkowski, The Arizona Daily Star,
Tucson, Arizona, Mar. 22, 1995

• Kim Peek shuffles slowly down a hallway at Cholla High School, his hands rubbing together, his head cocked to the side in a way that seems strangely familiar.

The resemblance becomes clear when he begins to speak, reciting dates, places and other trivia in a deep, distracting monotone: This is "Rain Man."

Of course, that's not quite right. It would be more accurate to say that "Rain Man"—the nickname of the character portrayed by Dustin Hoffman in the movie—is Kim Peek . . .

THE REAL 'RAIN MAN' KIM PEEK,
INSPIRATION FOR MOVIE, SHARES HIS
INSPIRED KNOWLEDGE
*by Kathrin Chavez, Observer-Dispatch,
Utica, New York, Apr. 28, 1995*

• . . . His brain configuration is so abnormal he should have died in infancy, but instead it gave him special gifts he now shares with whomever will listen to his message . . .

• Last night, he was the keynote speaker for the Abilities Awareness Dinner sponsored by Friends in Deed of the Retarded Foundation . . . a benefactor of The Arc of Oneida County.

But yesterday and today, he is spreading his message at area schools.

New York Mills students were hesitant when Peek's father invited them to ask his son questions.

Then Peek negotiated the stage steps on his father's arm and stood in front of them . . . and the students, disarmed by his extraordinary memory and his charming manner, soon were lining up to pepper him with questions.

"Tell me about Wilt Chamberlain's 100-point game."

"Name the British monarchs since the mid-1500s."

"Who were the losers of the last 10 Super Bowls?"

Questioned about clarinetist Benny Goodman by Senior Mike Loftus, Peek hummed Goodman's theme song "Let's Dance" and correctly identified his drummer as Gene Krupa.

He also listed the characters and quoted dialogue when student Jason Zebrowski asked him about "Macbeth," which the seniors are studying.

PEEK BRINGS SPECIAL TALENTS TO FORT DODGE
by Todd Dorman, The Messenger, Fort Dodge,Iowa,
May 25, 1995

• Kim Peek is warm, honest, outgoing and never at a loss for words.

Beyond the miracle of his abilities, he has the magic of Hollywood to thank . . .

• At a press conference upon his arrival . . . Peek showed off his skills in a display of Iowa historical knowledge . . .

Without pause, he recited historical facts about Iowa's first railroads in 1867. He sang "76 Trombones" from a musical by Iowa native Meredith Wilson.

Unprompted, he belted out the theme song to a John Wayne movie and correctly identified Wayne's Winterset home. On subjects from the Bible to sports, Peek is a walking encyclopedia.

"I read books in the morning and in the evening," Peek said. "I go to the libraries in the afternoons."

ANSWER MAN 'DIFFERENT'—AND AMAZING
BRAIN DEFECT NO HANDICAP TO AGILE MIND
by Thomas R. O'Donnell, The Des Moines Register,
Des Moines, Iowa, May 26, 1995

• . . . Kim Peek is a slightly rotund, extraordinarily friendly person who isn't afraid to give big hugs to complete strangers. His abilities drew "oohs" and "aahs" Thursday from groups ranging from high-school and middle-school students to business people.

Speaking in a steady, almost monotone voice, Peek answers a broad variety of questions, sometimes giggling or bursting into song when a query concerned music.

What movie won the most Oscars, and who starred in it?
"Ben Hur, Charlton Heston, in 1959," Peek said.
When did the Baltimore Colts win the Super Bowl?
"1979, under Don McCafferty."
Who was backup quarterback behind Johnny Unitas?
"Earl Morrall" . . .

• When the Peeks appear before an audience, "a lot of times it starts out like a sideshow, but it doesn't finish that way," Fran Peek said. "There's a lot of respect from the kids . . . They see it's OK to be different."

'RAIN MAN' BREAKS OUT OF SHELL
REAL-LIFE INSPIRATION FOR MOVIE NOW GIVES TALKS, DEMONSTRATING HIS AMAZING MEMORY OF FACTS, FIGURES AND URGING TOLERANCE
Associated Press, Rocky Mountain News, Greeley, Colorado, July 19, 1995

• . . . Brain damage during fetal development left Peek with diminished motor skills but gave him remarkable memory capacities.

Ask him who won the 1938 Academy awards:

"It was *You Can't Take it With You*—best picture; Spencer Tracy, *Boys Town*—best actor; Bette Davis, *Jezebel*—best actress," Peek replied without hesitation.

He can give the same immediate information on more than a dozen subjects . . .

• The attention the movie brought Peek has broken him out of his shell. The old Peek would avoid physical contact with people and often stand in a corner, facing the wall.

After *Rain Man,* he began to respond to others...

"He's getting a little bit of an ego now. He didn't have that before," [his] father said.

KIM PEEK HAS THE MIND OF A COMPUTER
by Crystal Pugsley, Plainsman, Sioux Falls,
South Dakota, Oct. 8, 1995

• . . . Shortly after his son's birth, doctors advised Peek and his wife to place their firstborn in an institution . . .

"We wouldn't let them do that," [Fran] Peek said. "He was a very needy child, he needed a lot of love and attention. Because his head was so large his neck muscles could not hold his head erect. We had to hold him until he was 3."

While doctors gave little hope that Kim would ever function normally, Peek said they were determined to provide every opportunity to learn.

When he was about 14 months old, they began reading to him. Cradling Kim in their arms, they would take his small finger and follow along the line they were reading, pointing to each word as they spoke . . .

"He was about 3 years old when he looked up the word *confidential* in the dictionary and read us the definition," [Fran Peek] said. "He had been reading newspapers on and off, but we thought he was just looking at pictures.

"We think that in reading to him when he was small and letting him follow the lines, he was developing photographic recall and learning how the words sounded . . .

"Barry found out how deep his knowledge was," Peek added. "We thought we knew him, but that's what happens in an overprotective environment."

• [Later, Dustin] Hoffman made Peek promise that he would allow Kim to leave the closet of his home environment and overcome his inhibitions and fear of people.

After "Rainman" . . . Peek decided it was time to honor the promise . . .

"We didn't want it to look like it was exploiting his talent, so we've never charged any fee for anything, just expenses if we're away from home . . ."

WITH THE HELP OF KIM PEEK . . .
THE ASSOCIATION FOR RETARDED CITIZENS
WILL HONOR A GROUP OF DESERVING VOLUNTEERS
THIS WEEK WITH A . . . SHOWER OF GRATITUDE
by E'Louise Ondash, Times Advocate, San Diego, California,
Oct. 15, 1995

• . . . Kim's San Diego appearance is the latest in a long speaking itinerary that began in 1989. It was Dustin Hoffman who, after spending several days with Kim, urged his family to "share Kim with the world."

• Once he started interacting with the public, "it was remarkable how he started to change," Fran said. "His social skills improved and he became adept at talking to people. He used to look away from people, but now he looks them in the eye."

• . . . At any rate, he keeps his father busy. Kim works two days a week as a payroll clerk (without the benefit of a calculator) at a community center for people with disabilities, and spends much of his remaining time honoring the speaking engagements.

"It's a full-time job for me and I'm getting older," said Fran, who owned an advertising agency before retiring in 1991, "but he never gets tired."

THE REAL RAIN MAN
by Patti Conley, The Times, Beaver County, Pennsylvania,
Oct. 29, 1995

• . . . When Kim talks, his father is the glue who fills in the gaps, who gently interprets Kim's seemingly disjointed facts and helps link his associations into the compelling chunks of information they are . . .

• Kim is "kind of the warm part of my heart," his father says. "I tell everybody that he is first of all a very marvelous person . . ."

He can't dance, play softball or play the piano. But he has memorized every TV station in the United States by its call letters and numbers. Every year, *TV Guide* sends him its fall premiere issue, which he reads and memorizes. He loves libraries.

• "Rain Man" called attention to people with disabilities and created interest in medical circles for brain research, Fran says. Their talks give parents of children who are mentally retarded and autistic hope . . .

• Drew Grivna . . . executive director of The Arc, Beaver County Chapter, has met Kim . . . twice at Arc functions . . .

This is not a "dog and pony" show during which Kim's recall abilities are illustrated merely for entertainment, Grivna says. "It presents an opportunity to meet someone who has different characteristics and an outlook that may be totally foreign to us."

Kim taking on all comers, 1991

Media Megabytes II

K IM WAS SUDDENLY THRUST INTO THE UNEXPECTED ROLE of local celebrity. The Utah State Board of Education and the Murray School District presented him his high school diploma; Utah State University's College of Education selected him as its Honorary Valedictorian for 1992; and many civic and volunteer organizations have since honored him for his "respect-others-and-be-the-best-you-can-be" quest.

In July of 1993, a crew from ABC News's *20/20* came to Salt Lake to shoot a segment about how Kim had changed since the movie's release. They had heard about Kim from a newspaper article covering a visit we made to Casper, Wyoming, where he spoke to ten schools in four days. The feature was broadcast nationally in January, 1994, followed by an appearance later that year on *Good Morning, America*.

Following is a brief summary of comments taken from these two telecasts:

20/20, JANUARY 7, 1994 WITH HOSTS
*Hugh Downs and Barbara Walters,
and special correspondent Bob Brown
(The broadcast included interviews with Kim, Barry Morrow,
Dr. Dan Christensen, and me, along with clips from the movie and
from Kim's presentations.)*

•[Downs] It was the movie that won all the big categories at the Academy Awards five years ago, best picture, best director, best actor. A stellar moment for everyone involved with the film *Rain Man*. But it was just a moment. Dustin

Hoffman long since moved on to other roles.

But what about the man whose life inspired that title character? Well, as you're about to see, years later the impact of his life is profound. Let Bob Brown introduce you to this remarkable person, the *real* Rain Man . . .

•[Brown] In his mind is a treasury of facts and riddles . . . His father will tell you that, if he has read something, he seems to remember it always, even though tests measure his I.Q. at around 70 . . .

Kim Peek, 42 years old, is one of those rare people known as savants, who by one measure can barely function without full time care and who may seem emotionally removed from the rest of the world. But they also have astonishing, unexplained gifts for performing complex mathematics in their heads, or, in Kim's case, memorizing facts . . .

•[Barry Morrow] You know, most of us, we present our best sides right away. With Kim it's all backwards. Immediately you see the eccentric things, the things that are kind of wrong or slightly different. And then it's over time, the genius, the gift, the goodness reveals itself . . .

•[Brown] When Morrow then created the character influenced by Kim in *Rain Man*, that was in one sense the beginning of Kim's coming out. He went to Hollywood. He met movie stars . . . He seemed suddenly to flourish amid all the attention he got . . .

Kim was disruptive in school, and so he was kept for much of his early life among the books in his home and in his room . . .

• [Dr. Christensen, showing scans of Kim's brain alongside those of a normal brain] . . . Kim's head is simply much bigger than the average head. And a band of tissue that's present at this point in most all of us, the corpus callosum actually connecting the left and right hemispheres . . . well, I challenge you to find one . . .

Why a brain that looks so disfigured and in some ways functions better than mine is a mystery . . .

•[Brown] You may remember that at the end of *Rain Man* the character played by Dustin Hoffman is returned to institutional care . . . Knowing Kim, the ending, says Barry Morrow, is one thing he might do differently today.

• [Morrow] We have to revise our thinking that Kim or his equivalent, Raymond Babbitt, should be in an institution. I don't think anybody could spend five minutes with Kim and not come away with a slightly altered view of themselves, the world, and our potential as human beings.

• [Walters] You know, Bob, Kim is considered retarded, yet he can do things that few of us can do. We label people, and sometimes we make fun of people, and if there is a lesson, this is it.

Good Morning, America, August 4, 1994,
with host Joan Lunden
(This brief segment also included several clips from Kim's
presentations and interviews with Kim, Barry, and me.)

• [Lunden] . . . After the movie's enormous success, people became curious about the so-called *real* Rain Man. And so, Kim Peek, who inspired the story, came out of seclusion, and, with the help of his father, he began a career as a motivational speaker. And in the past six years Kim has appeared before hundreds of thousands of people, mostly school children. His message? That despite some people's outward differences, they, too, have something to contribute . . .

•[Lunden to me] I would imagine, Fran, that when they at first said there's no other choice other than institutionalization, even suggesting a lobotomy, I imagine you've been very protective over your lifetime of Kim. How's it been; has it been tough to let him go out there?

[Me] Sure, I think that's the biggest problem all parents have with children with disabilities. They overprotect them.

You've got to let them go out into the world, as Barry encouraged me to do, take him out into the world, let him have a chance to fail as well as succeed, to let him be a whole person, and that's what's happened with him . . .

A Final Word

THESE NATIONWIDE TV SEGMENTS STIMULATED EVEN more requests for Kim to travel and campaign for local chapters of The Arc. As of July, 1995, Kim has interacted with over half a million people (370,000 of them students) plus an ongoing combined TV audience of an estimated 80 million viewers since his "coming out" in March of 1989. He's warm, he's funny. And his outgoing personality and his special talents have touched the hearts and minds of many, as has his upbeat message: "Learning to recognize and respect differences in others and treating them as you want them to treat you will bring us the kind of world we want to live in. Let's share, care . . . and be our best!"

And we hope to continue to carry this quiet yet powerful message to hundreds of thousands more people in the years ahead. When I see audiences enthused and awed by Kim's abilities, his warmth and total trust, I know we made the right

Mingling, 1994

decision when we chose to share our message. Kim has received many awards, many standing ovations, many handshakes, many hugs, and thousands of notes and letters of appreciation for his appearances and what he does for others. He's a happy, healthy young man truly enjoying the 44-year mark in his life.

My life has dramatically changed, too. Still I keep Kim as top priority in everything we do. We are a team. We live together, work together, and plan together for tomorrow.

Many people ask: "What will become of Kim should something happen to you?" I really don't know. What the future holds is beyond my grasp. Instead we treat each day as it comes. His mother is very much a part of his life and his feelings; he visits her often, and she is always ready and willing to help. He also has a married brother with two young daughters who care very much about Kim. Kim's sister, Alison, owns her own business and also plays an indispensable role in his life and concerns. And, as already mentioned, we are blessed with hundreds of friendships.

Like everyone else, we have our down days. We struggle. But we also keep trying. With Kim's newfound determination and unbridled passion for life, what else can we do?

Still, some real, unknown tomorrows loom before us. But

at the same time, there are many helpful yesterdays to give us experience and countless present possibilities to enable us to move forward. Even now Kim is working on a project dealing with, of all things, plants. Furthermore, his reading interests are slowly beginning to branch out into new subject areas. So you never know what treasures might yet come out of the laboratory of his fertile, unassuming, quirky mind—a mind that has only quite recently become fully connected to his heart. Maybe Kim, as he continues to step out into his own, personal "brave new world," is just now hitting his stride. As he says: "Our tomorrows will be happy times."

Yes, Kim, Dustin was right when he said, " . . . You are the heavens!" If mankind would just incorporate into their lives the qualities that make you who and what you are, most of the world's problems would soon disappear.

Thank you, Kim, for making my heart overflow with love. I am so very proud of you. Dad loves you very much.

Sometimes we go nose to nose.